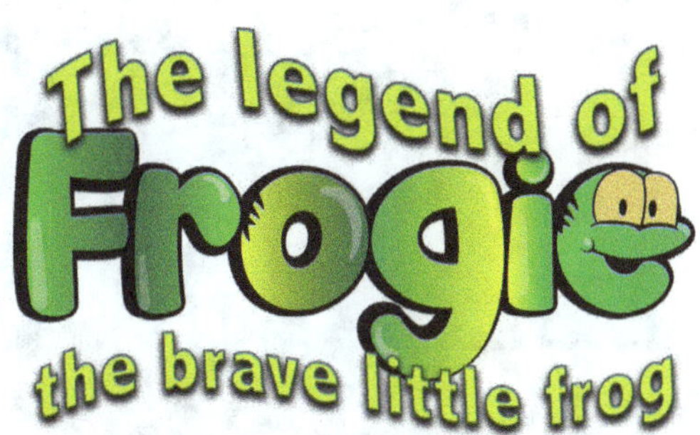

ISBN: 9798859751051

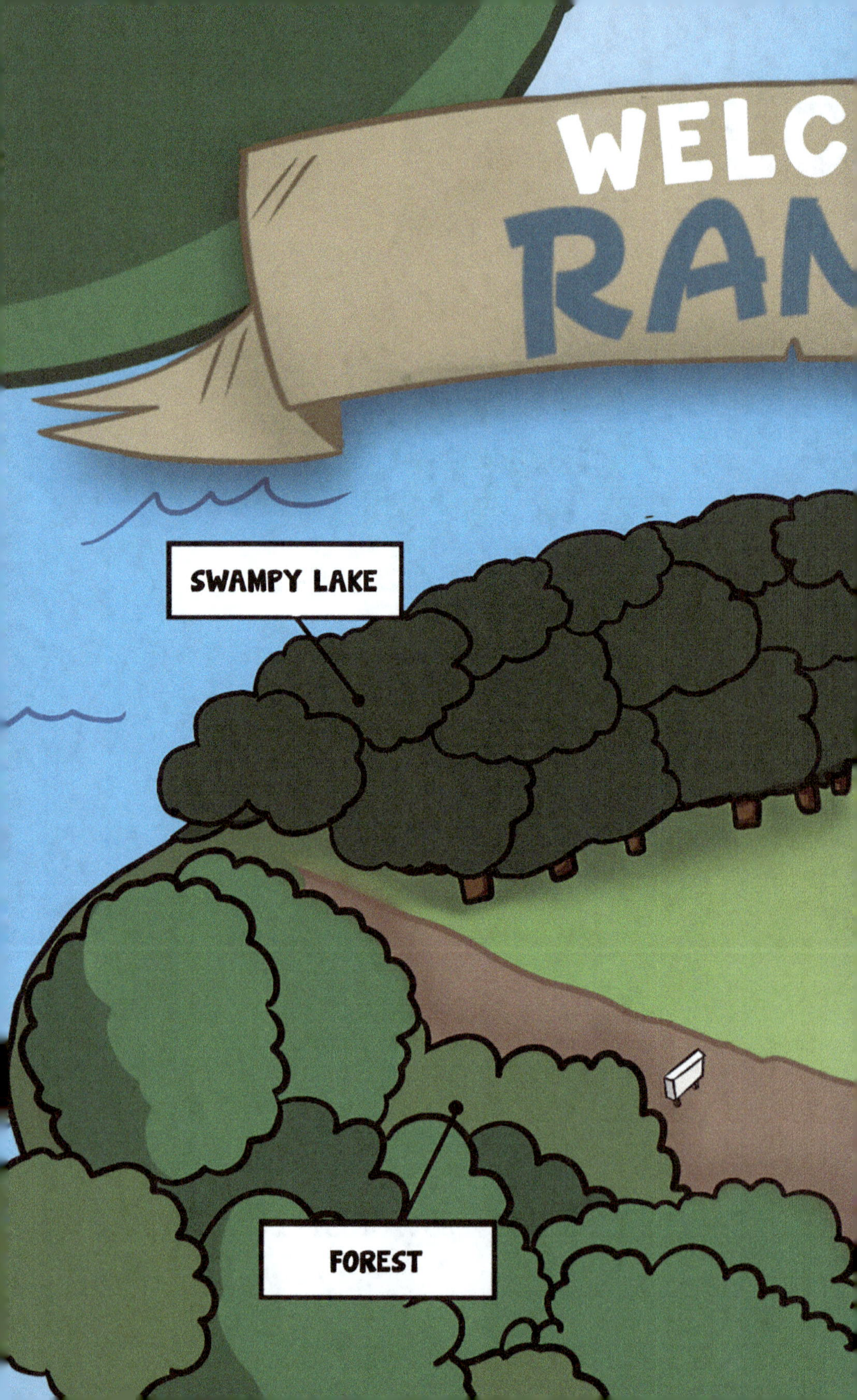

WELC
RAN
SWAMPY LAKE
FOREST

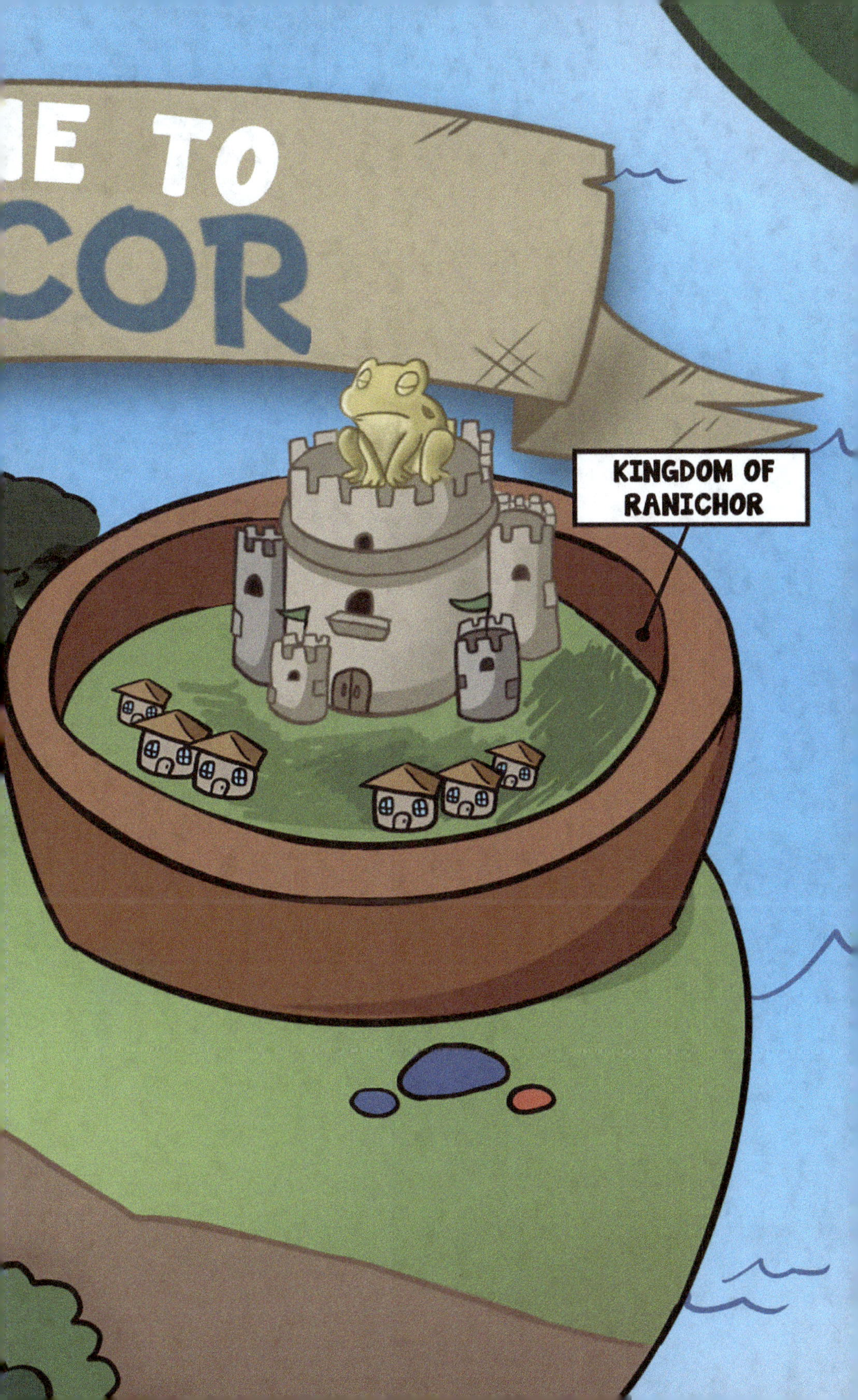

E TO
COR
KINGDOM OF RANICHOR

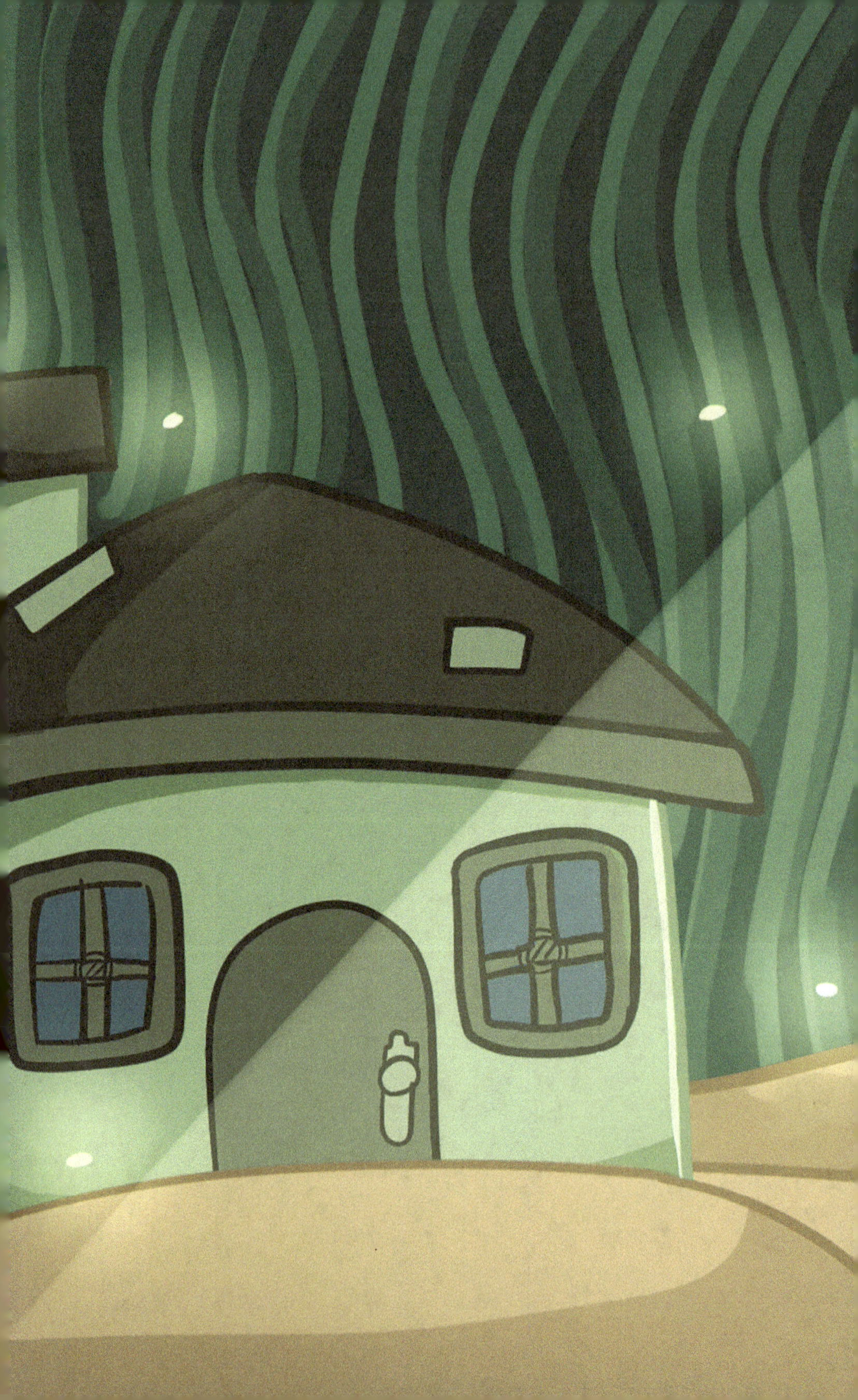

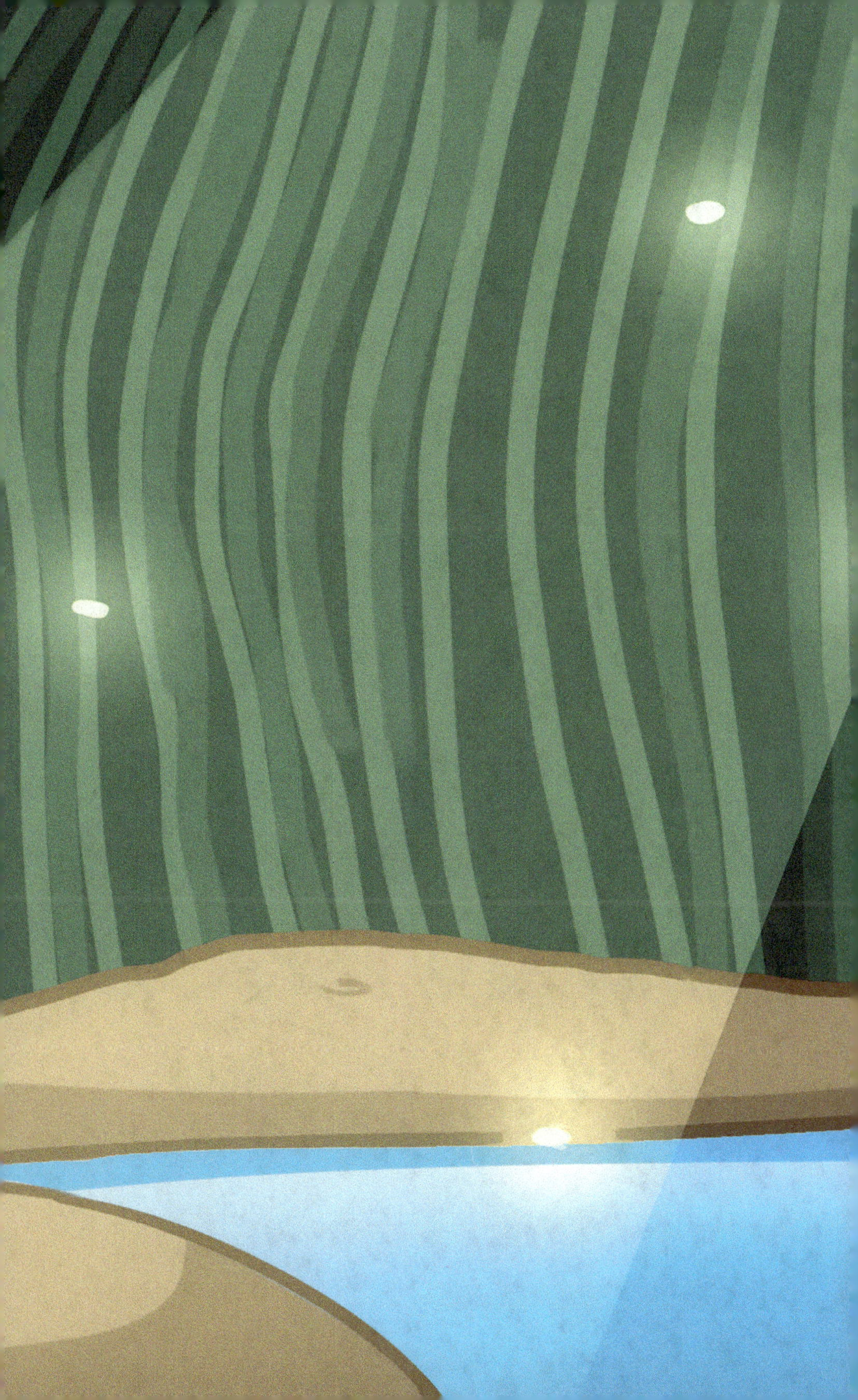

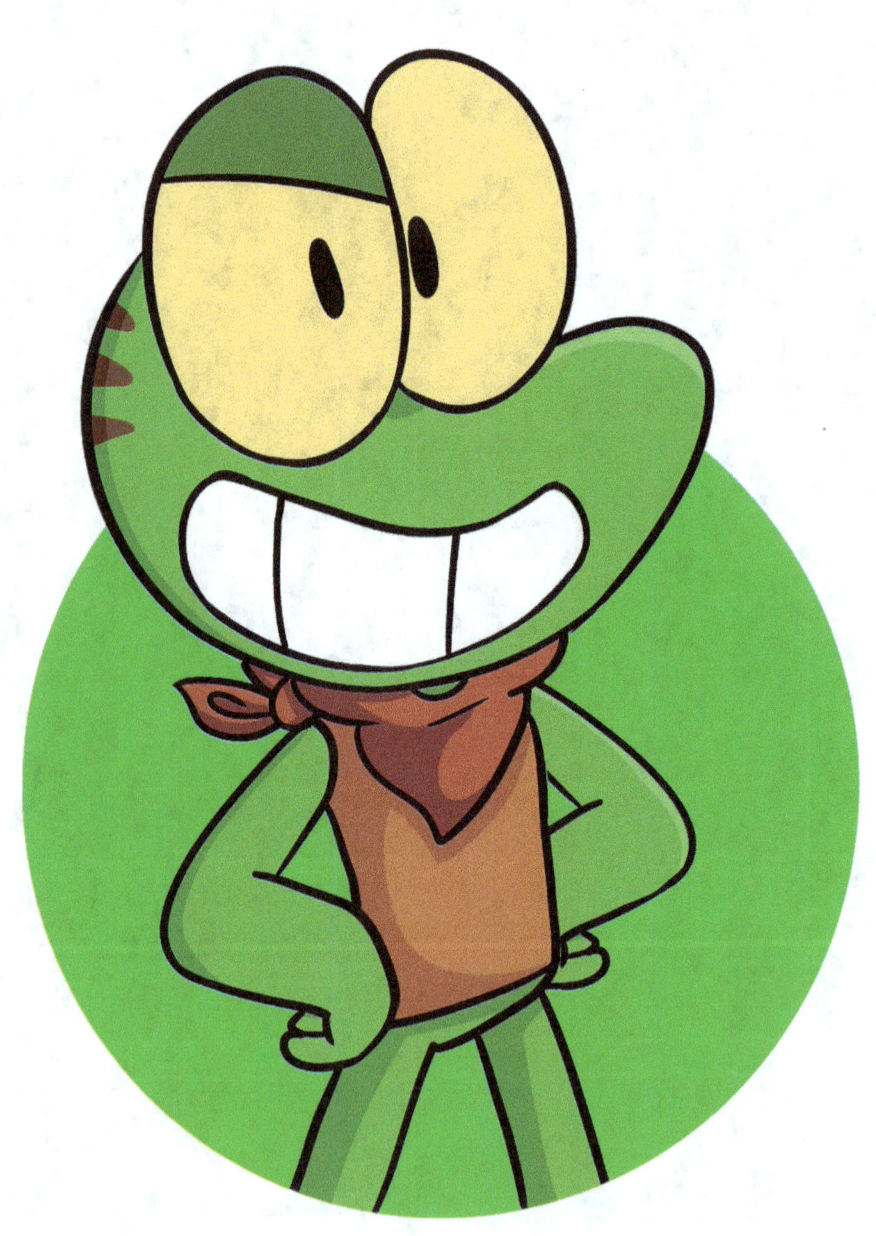

Frogie: He is an adventurous little bright green frog who lives in the peaceful kingdom of Ranicor. Despite her small size, Frogie has a big heart and a strong desire to become a hero.

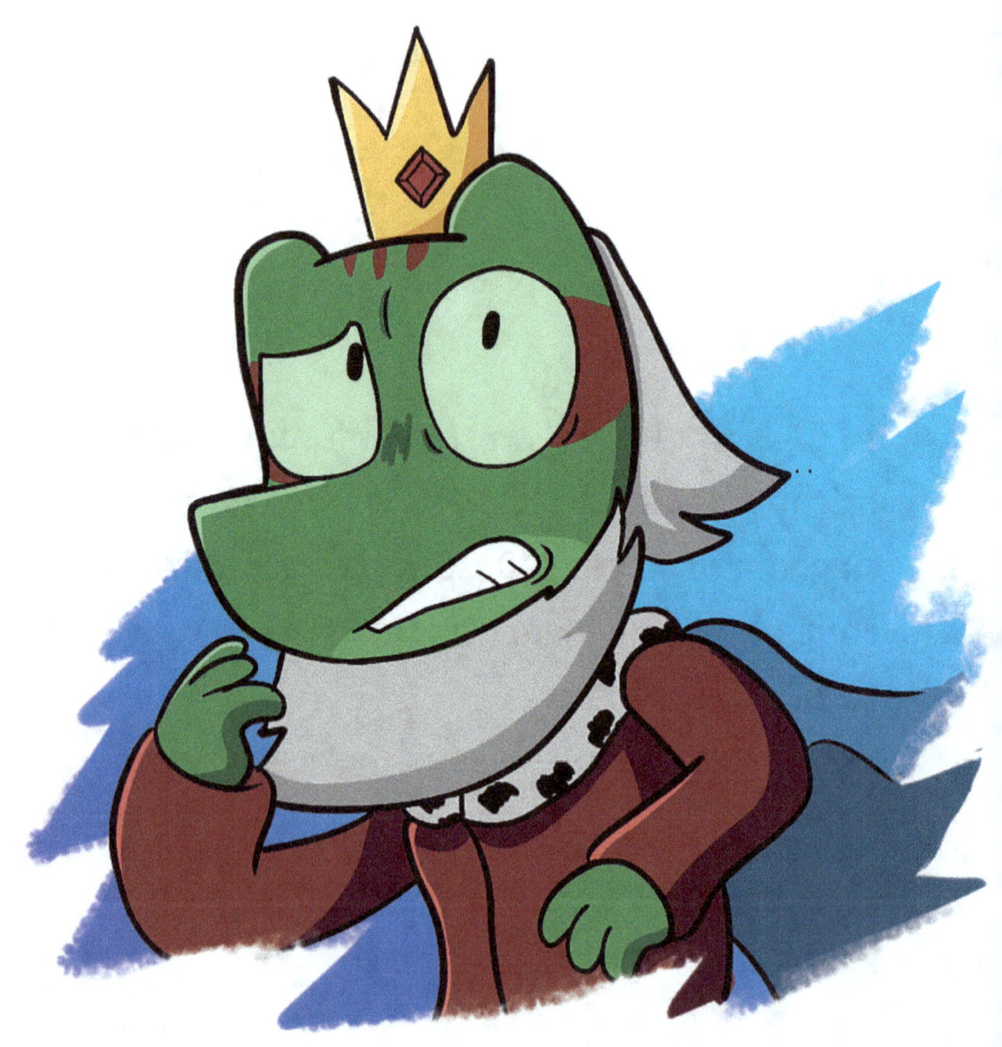

The King: Represents authority and leadership, concerned about how to protect his people from the dangers that surround his peaceful kingdom.

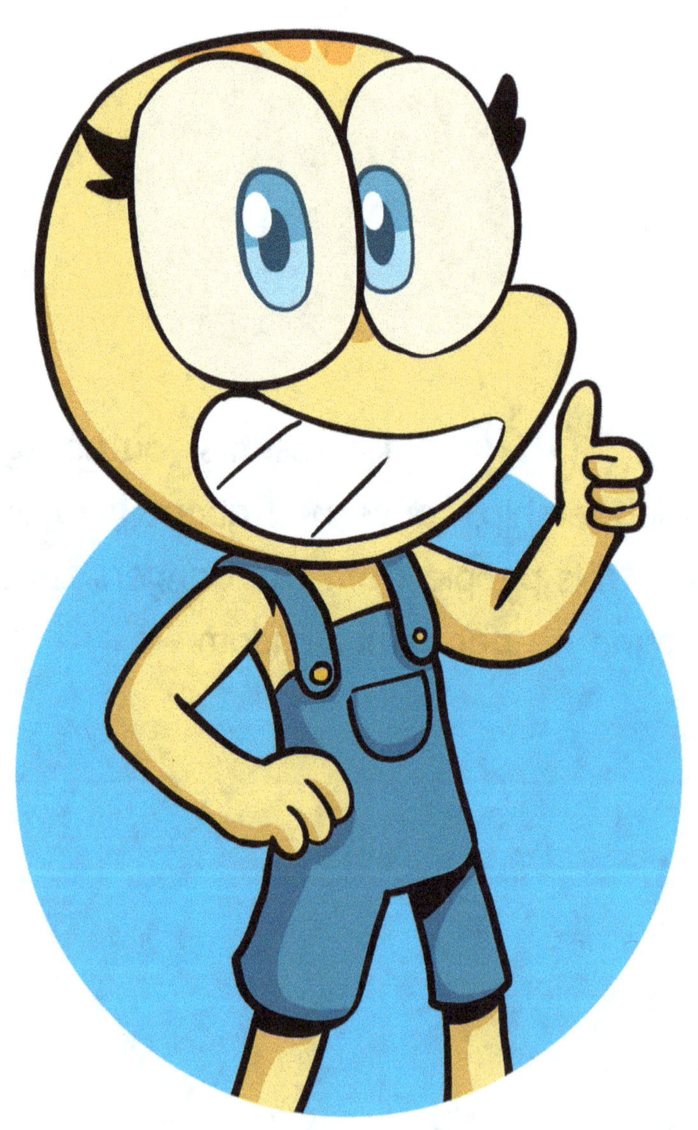

Laly: She is a yellow frog, a noble, vulnerable and shy young man that Frogie meets while exploring the kingdom, their friendship has no limits.

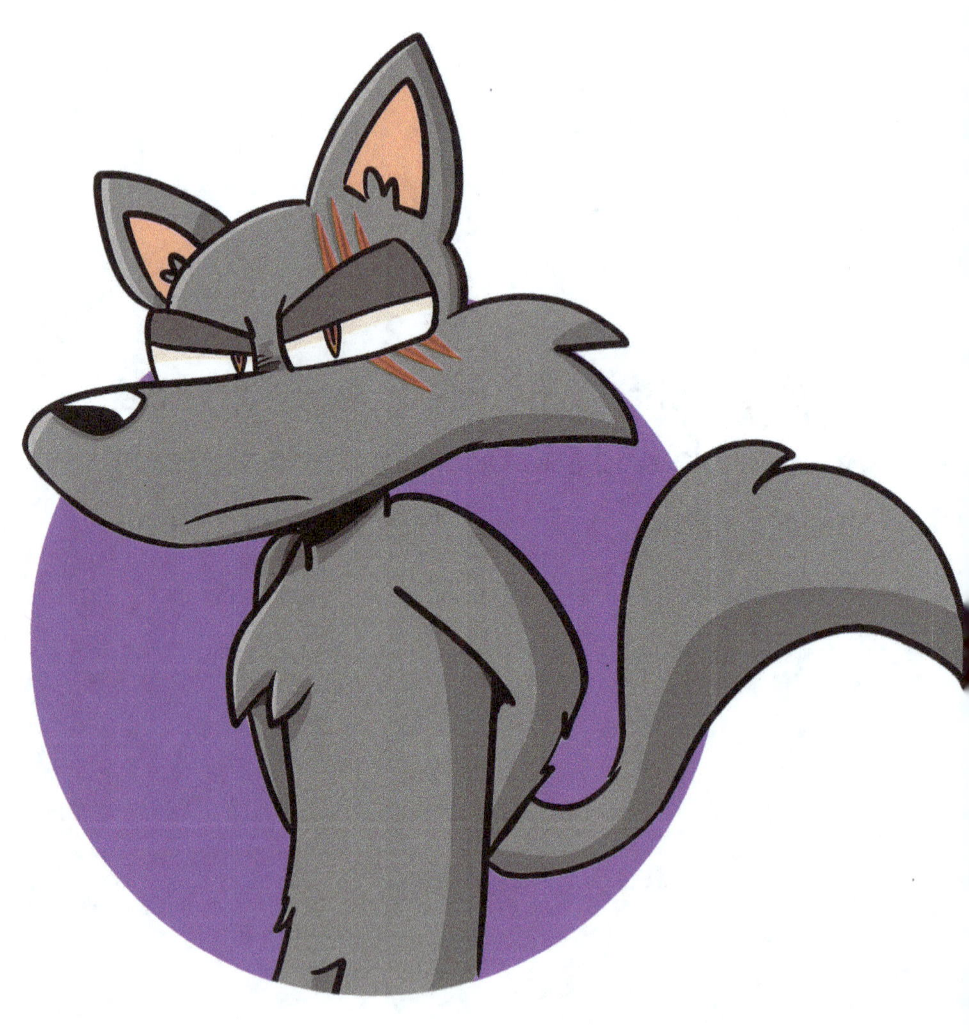

Scar: He is a cunning and fearsome coyote with a scar over his right eye. In the past, he had terrorized the peaceful kingdom of Ranicor, leaving a trail of destruction and fear.

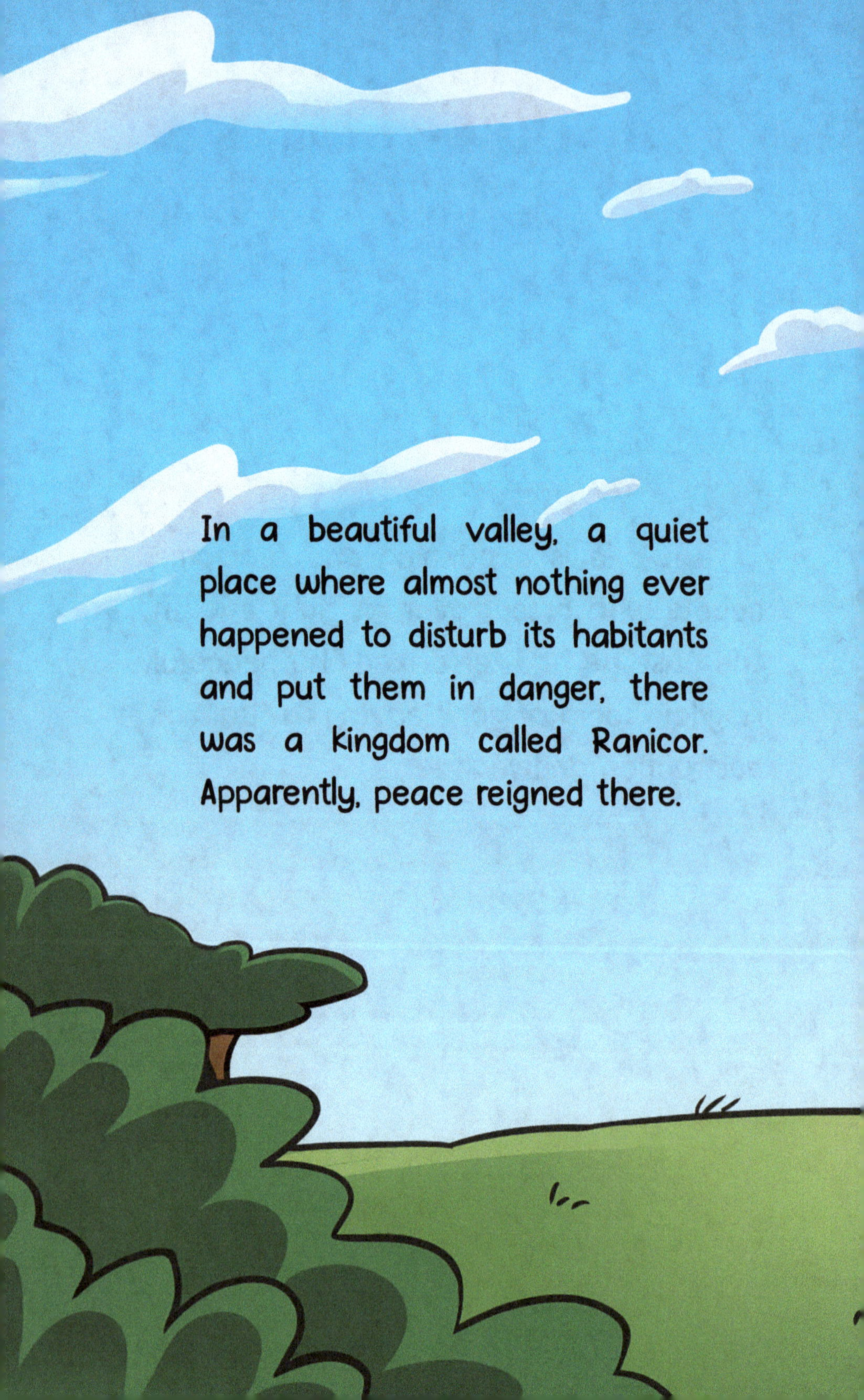

In a beautiful valley, a quiet place where almost nothing ever happened to disturb its habitants and put them in danger, there was a kingdom called Ranicor. Apparently, peace reigned there.

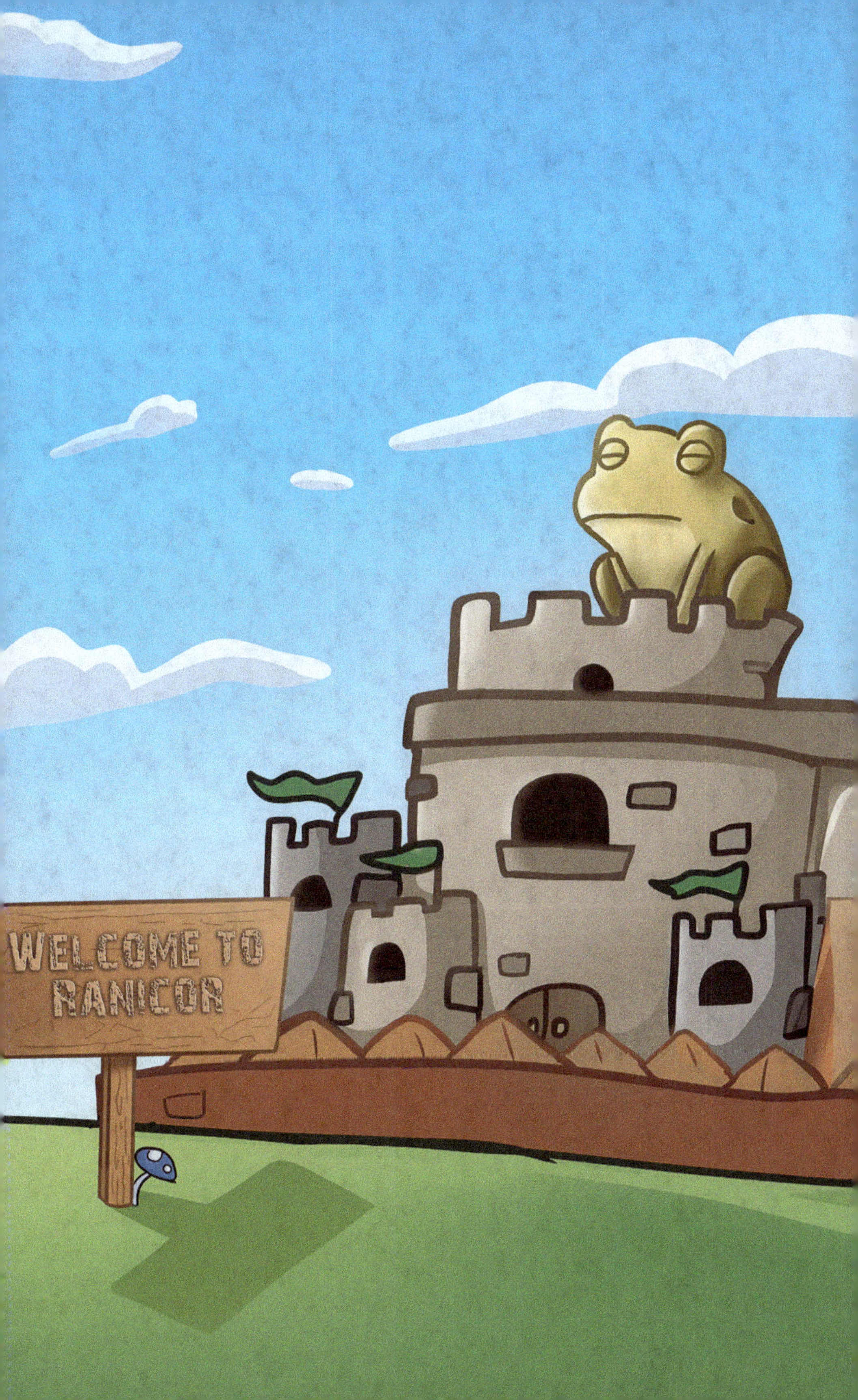

WELCOME TO
RANICOR

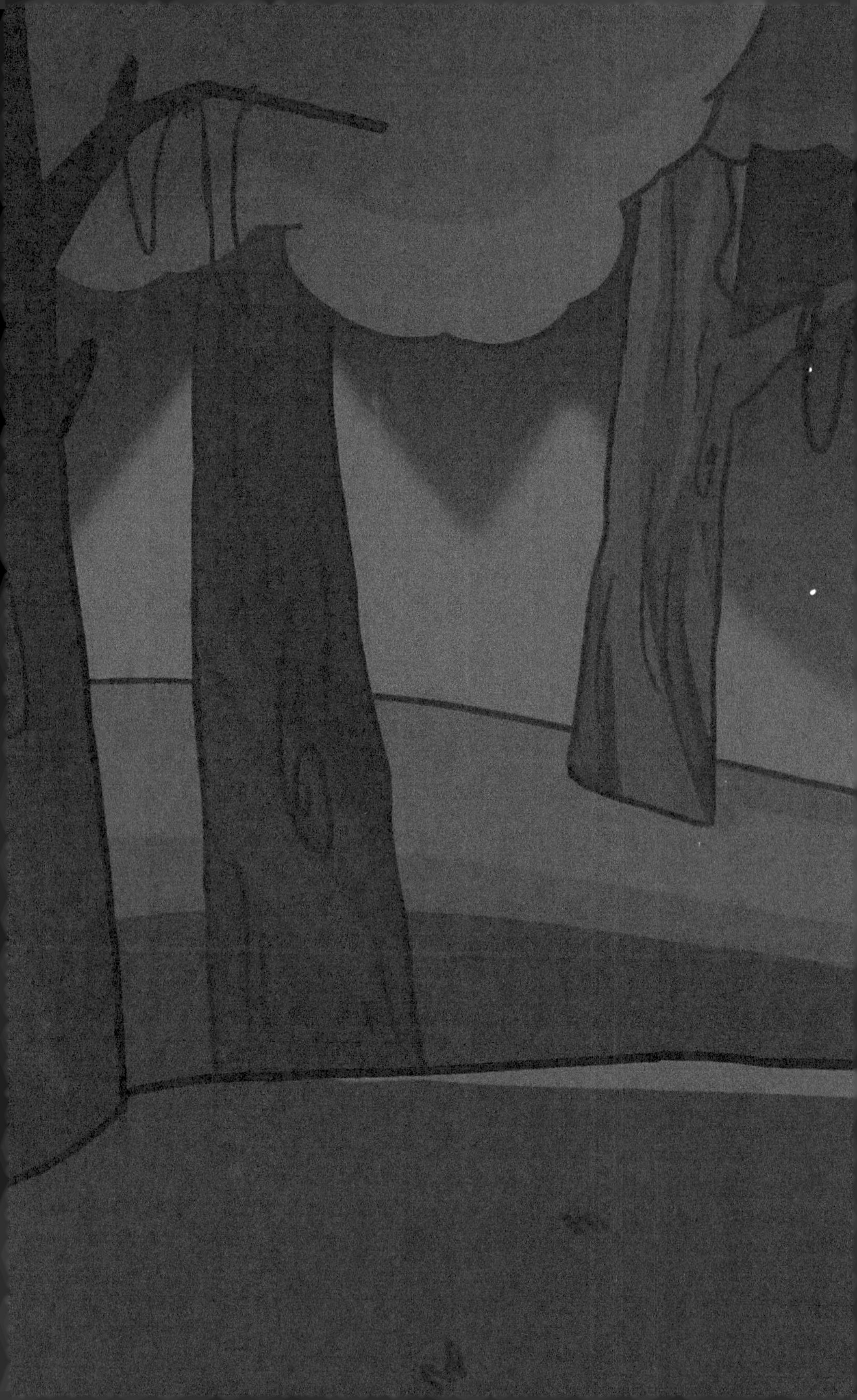

However, in the last days of that sunny summer, screams were heard at dawn and, the next day, remains of fallen branches and bushes were found as if they had seen some violent event. For this reason, the king of the Frogs remembered Scar, a coyote with a scar on his right eye.

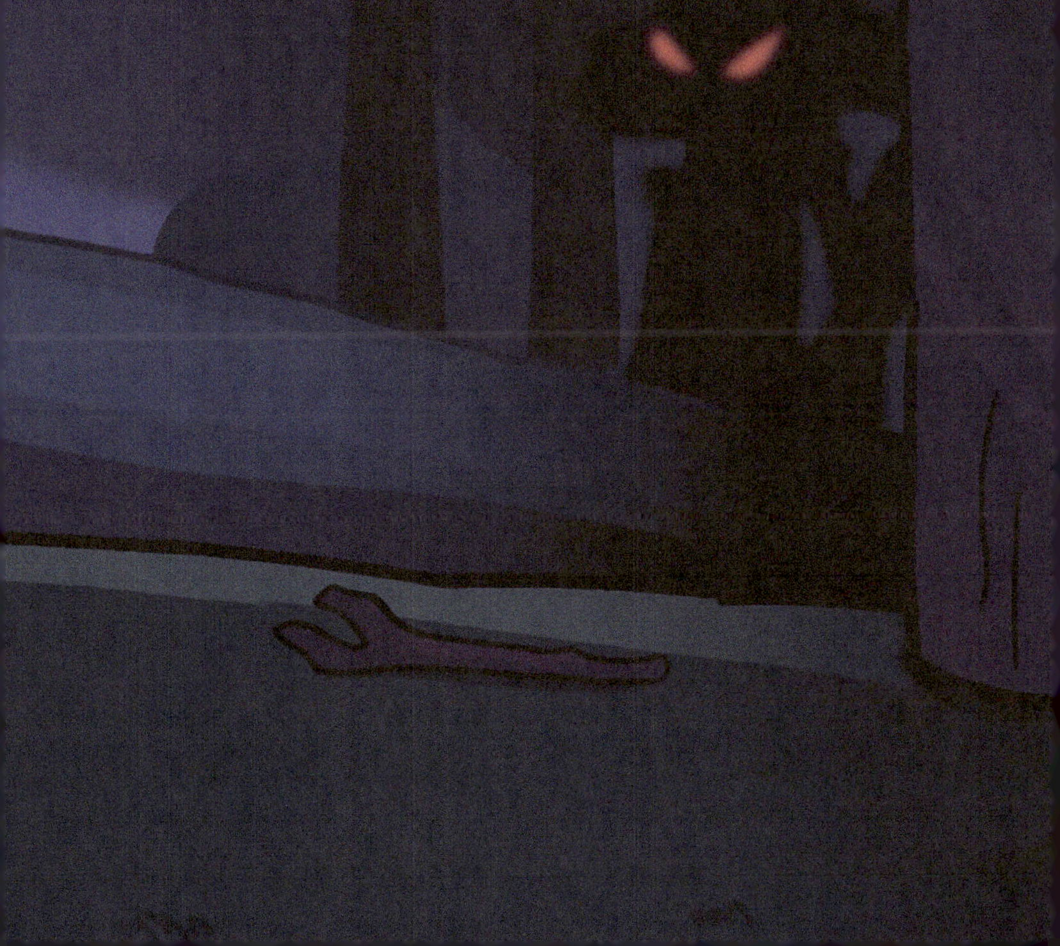

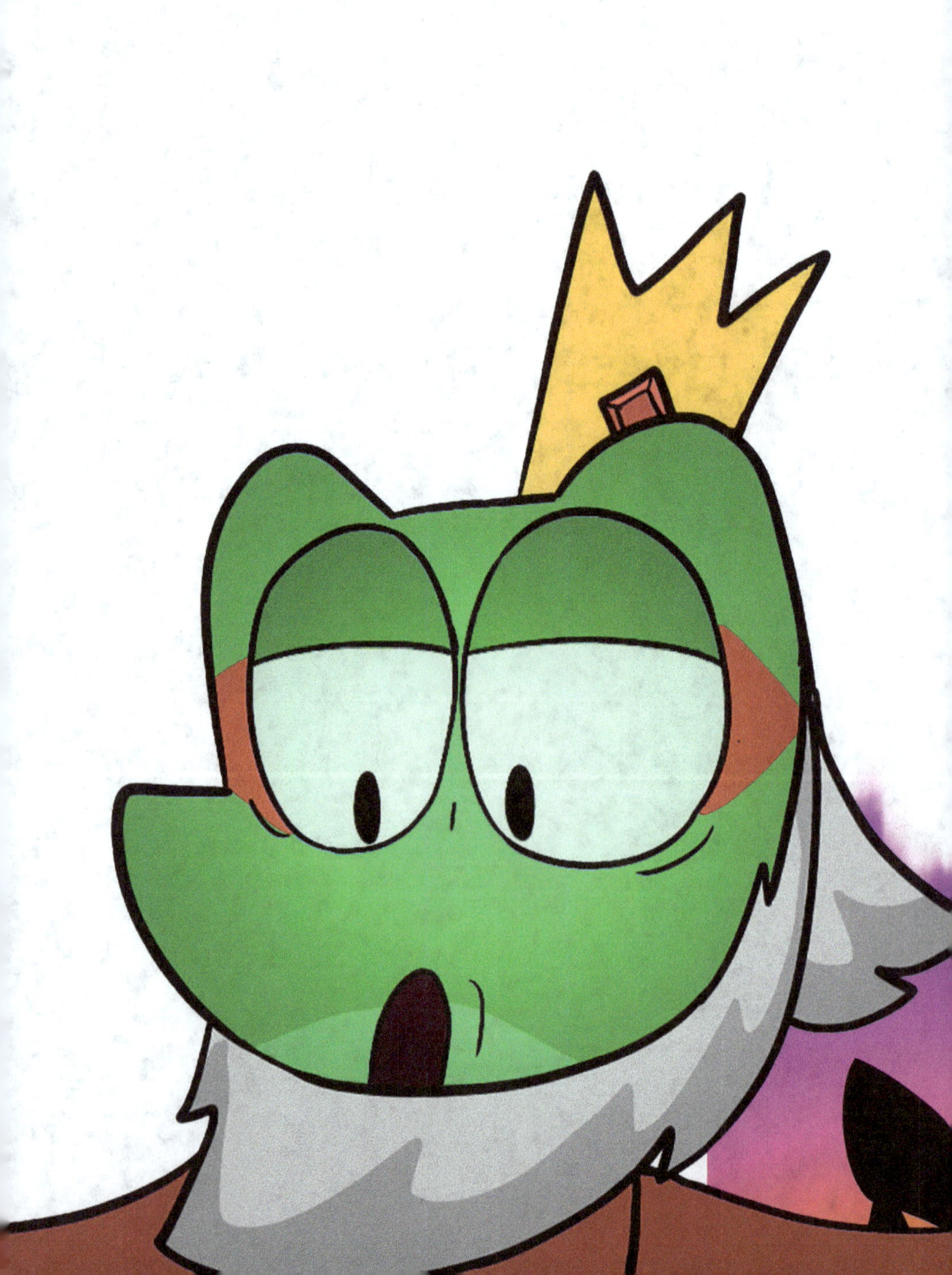

that years ago roamed the kingdom
stalking its habitants; and decided to
tell his subjects about him.

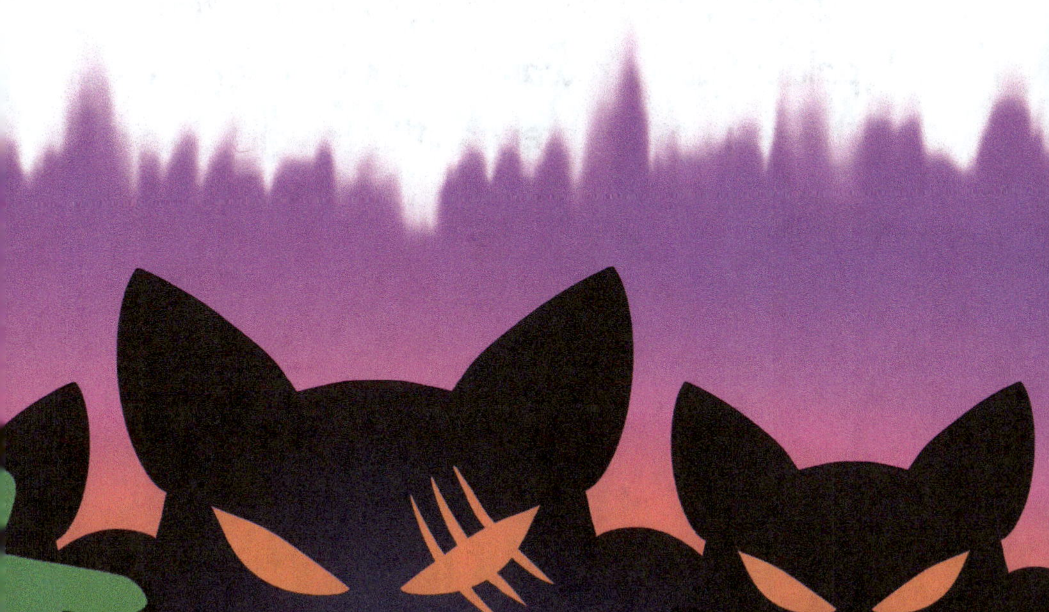

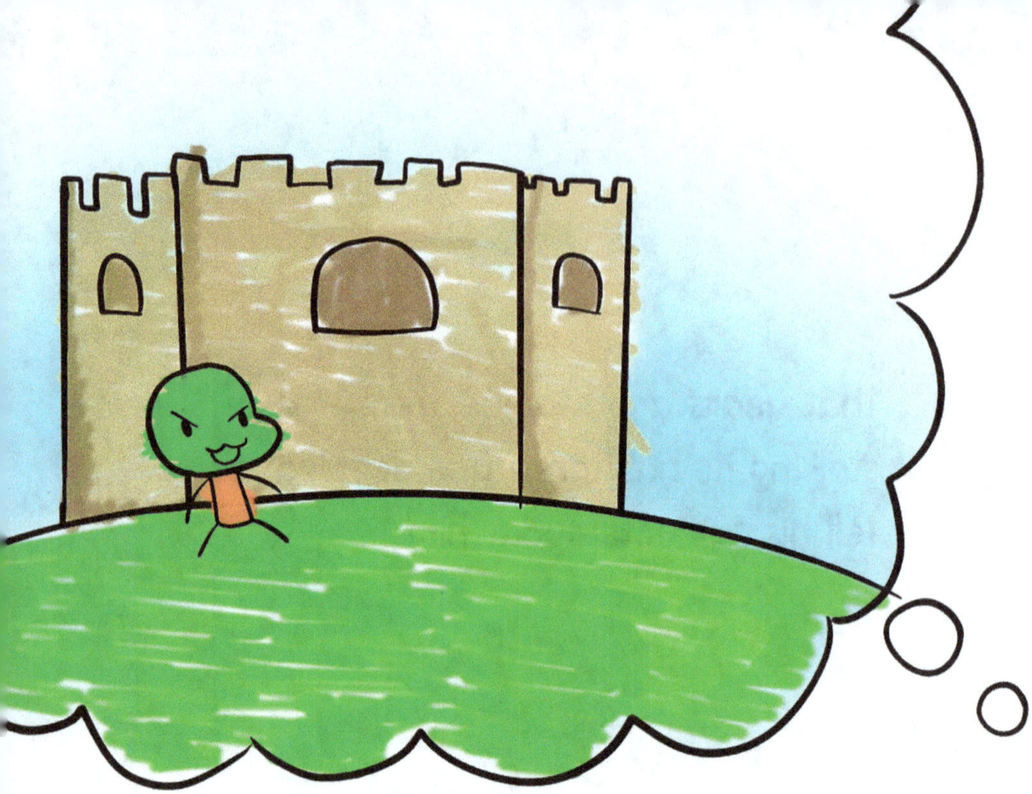

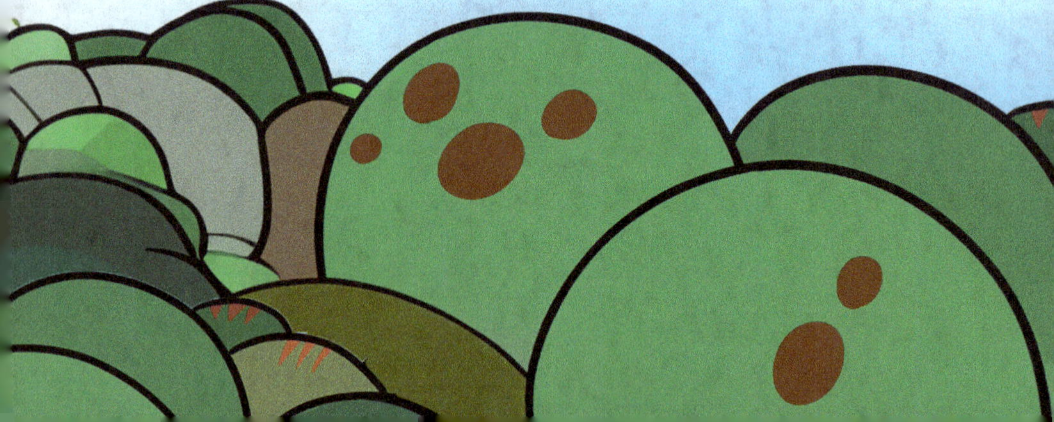

He also mentioned that Ranicor needed to free itself from the scourge of that coyote and decreed that only the bravest and strongest subject would be named a hero, would receive a beautiful palace as a reward and would enjoy the respect and recognition of all.

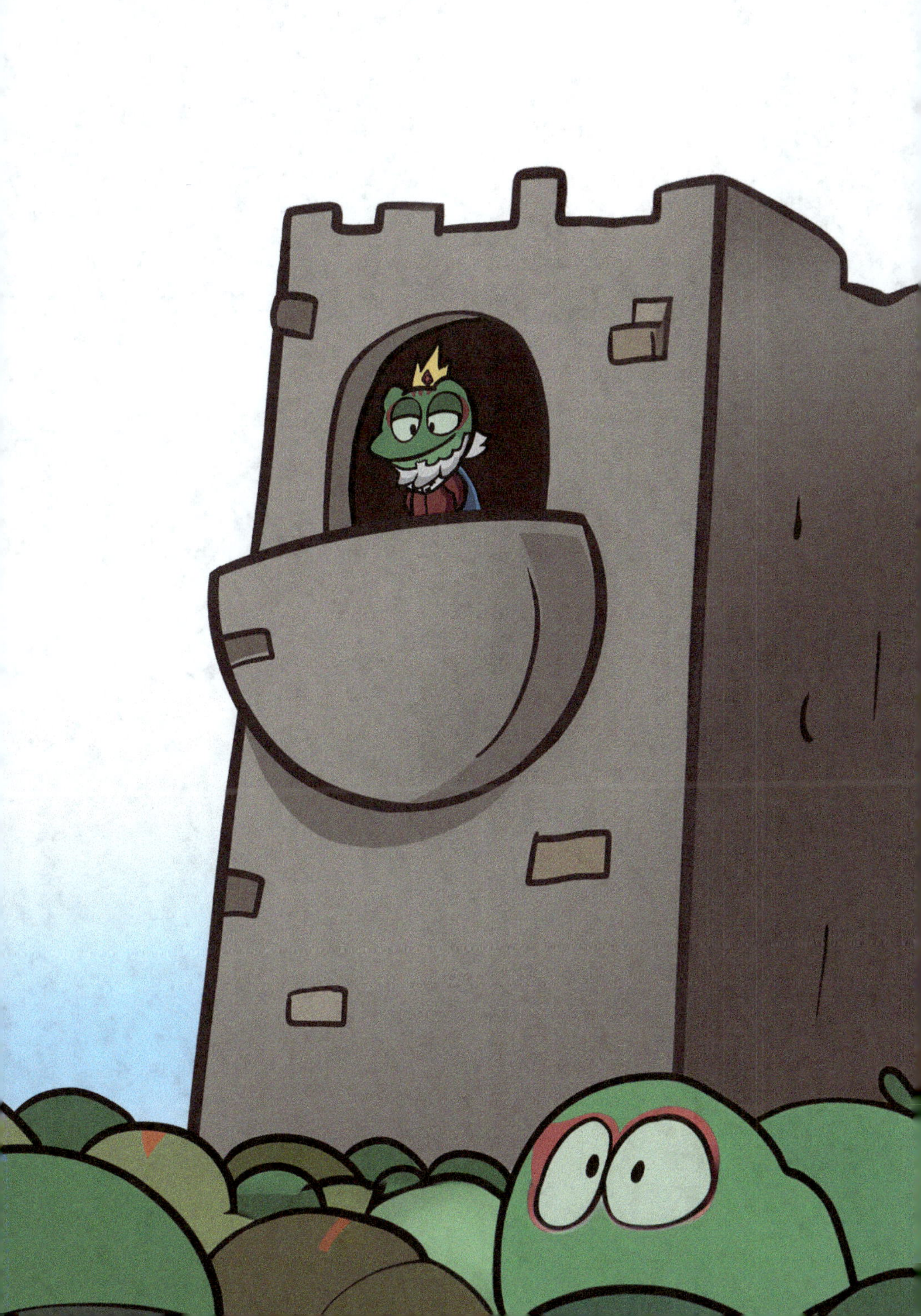

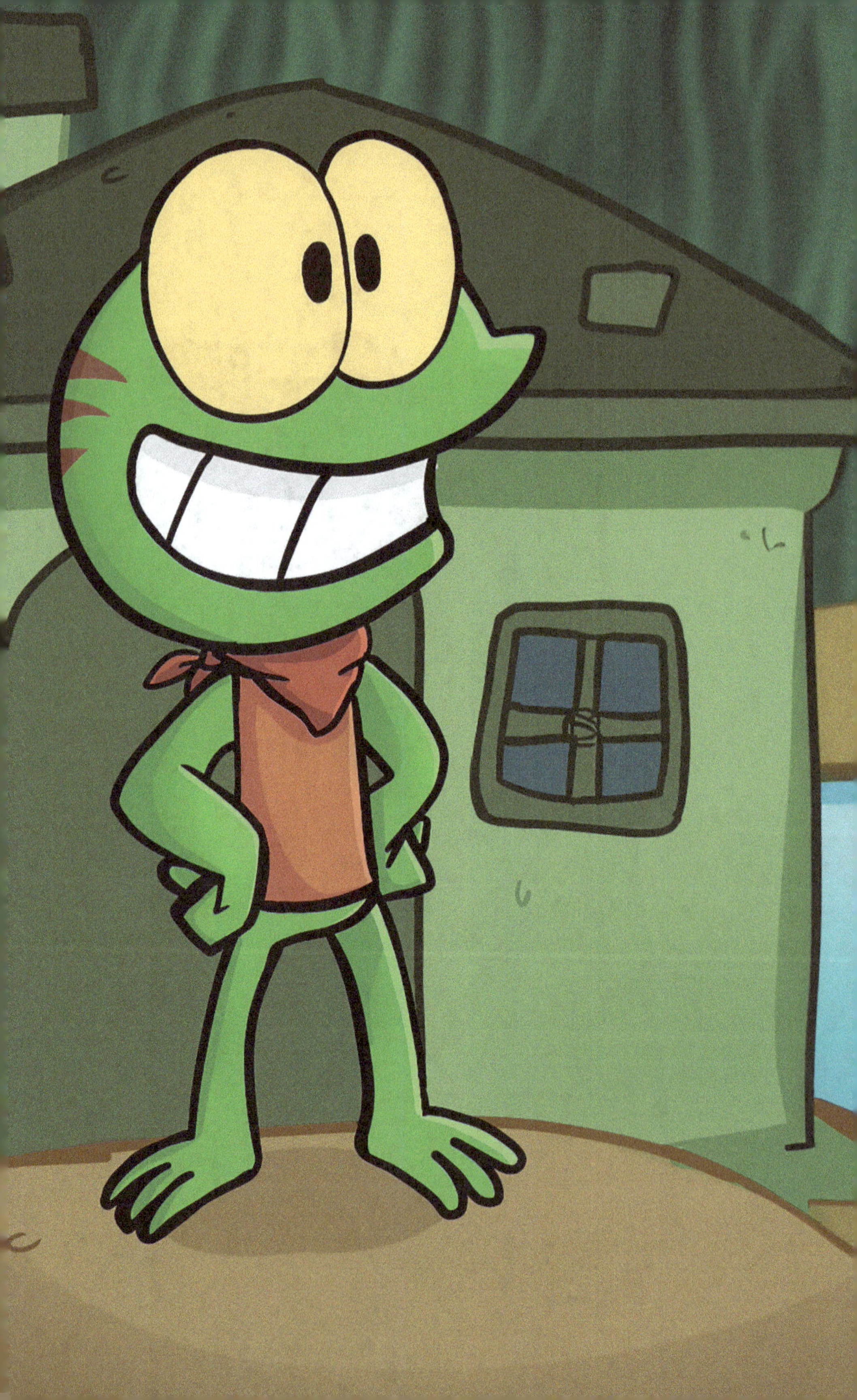

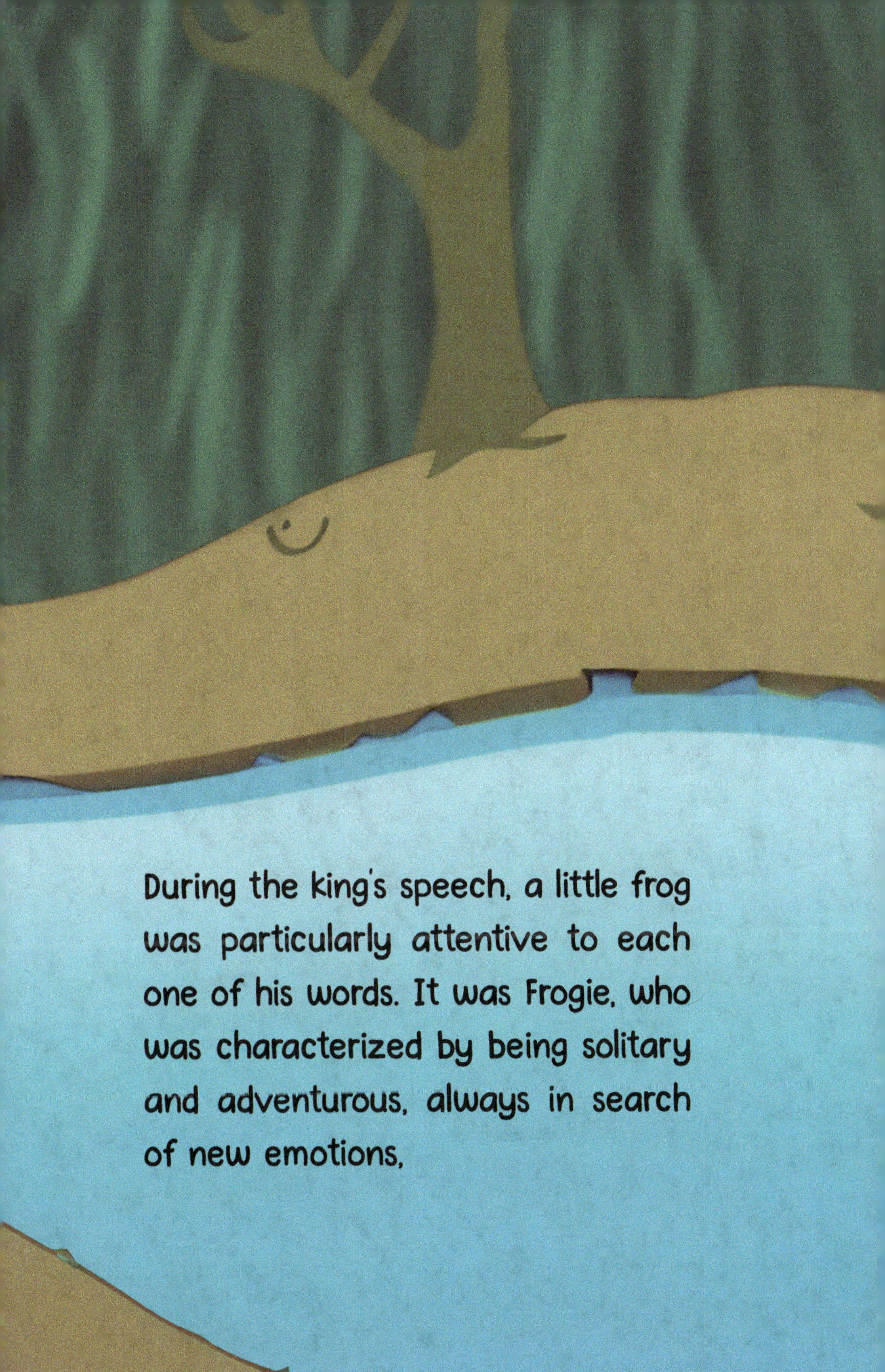

During the king's speech, a little frog was particularly attentive to each one of his words. It was Frogie, who was characterized by being solitary and adventurous, always in search of new emotions,

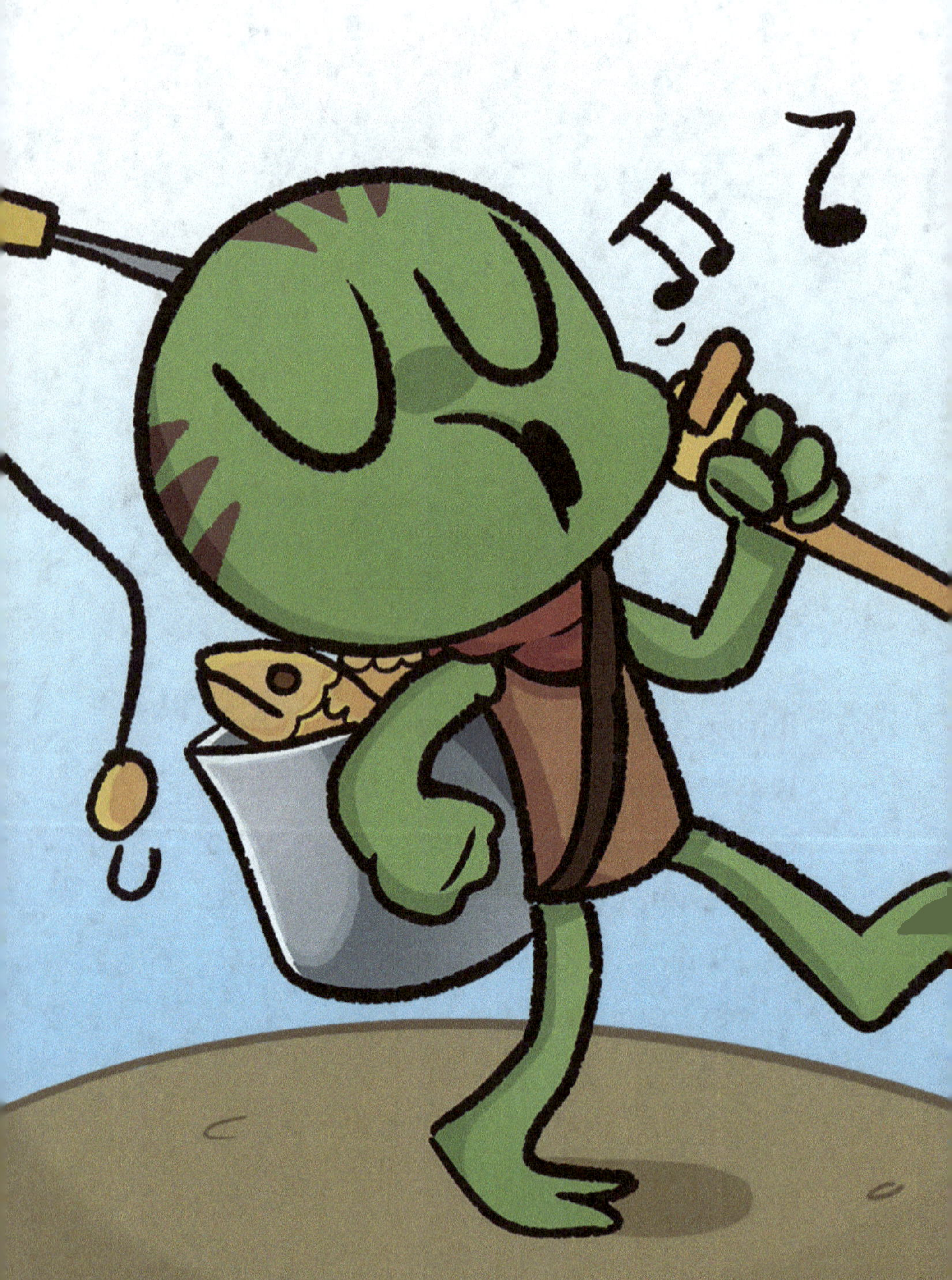

with his bright green color and his big jumping eyes, he dreamed of being a hero, saving his town from Scar's scourge, having everyone's respect and admiration, and living in a beautiful house.

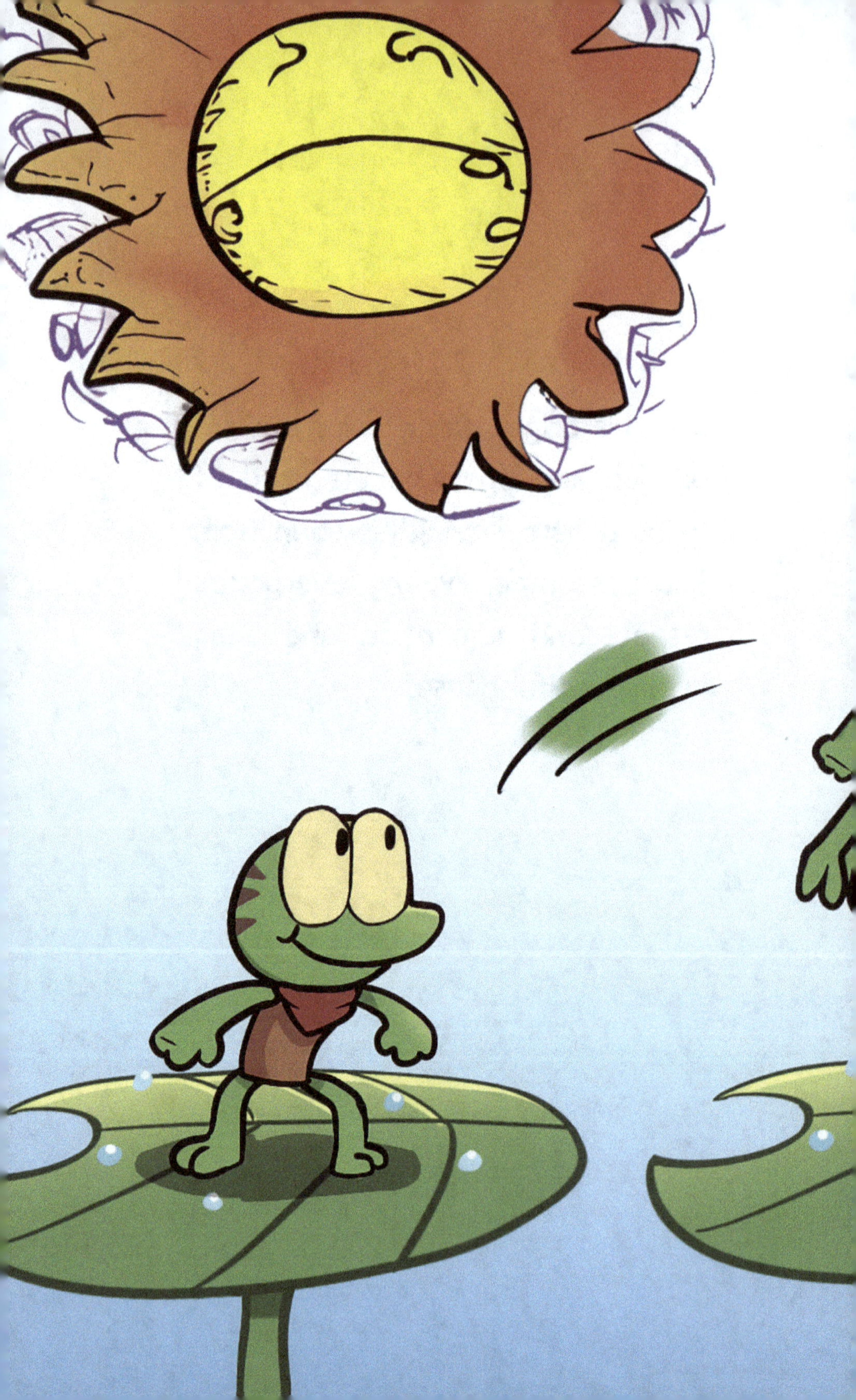

One sunny day, while Frogie was jumping from leaf to leaf, he heard a weak cry coming from a bush. He approached with curiosity and discovered a small scared frog covered with a dry leaf.

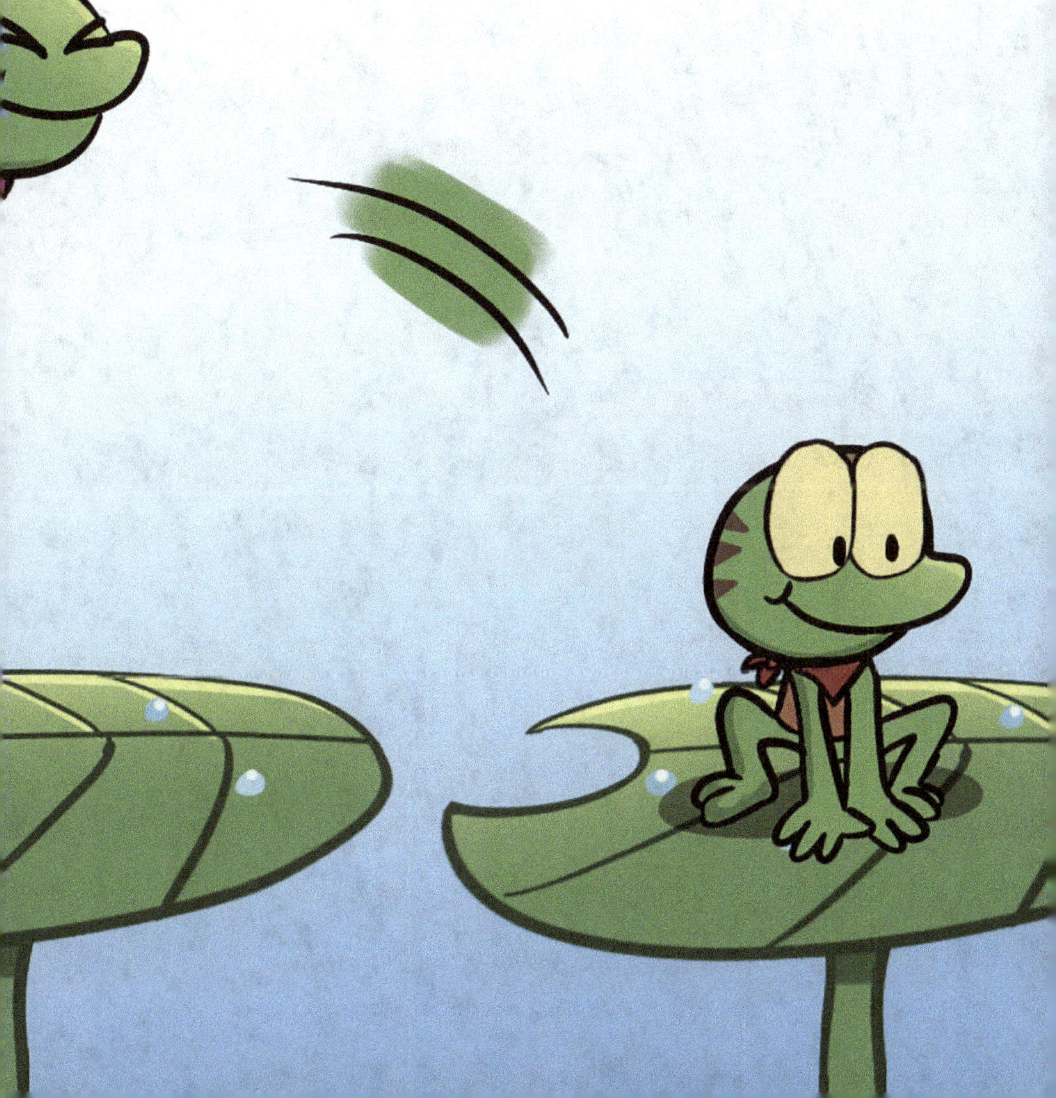

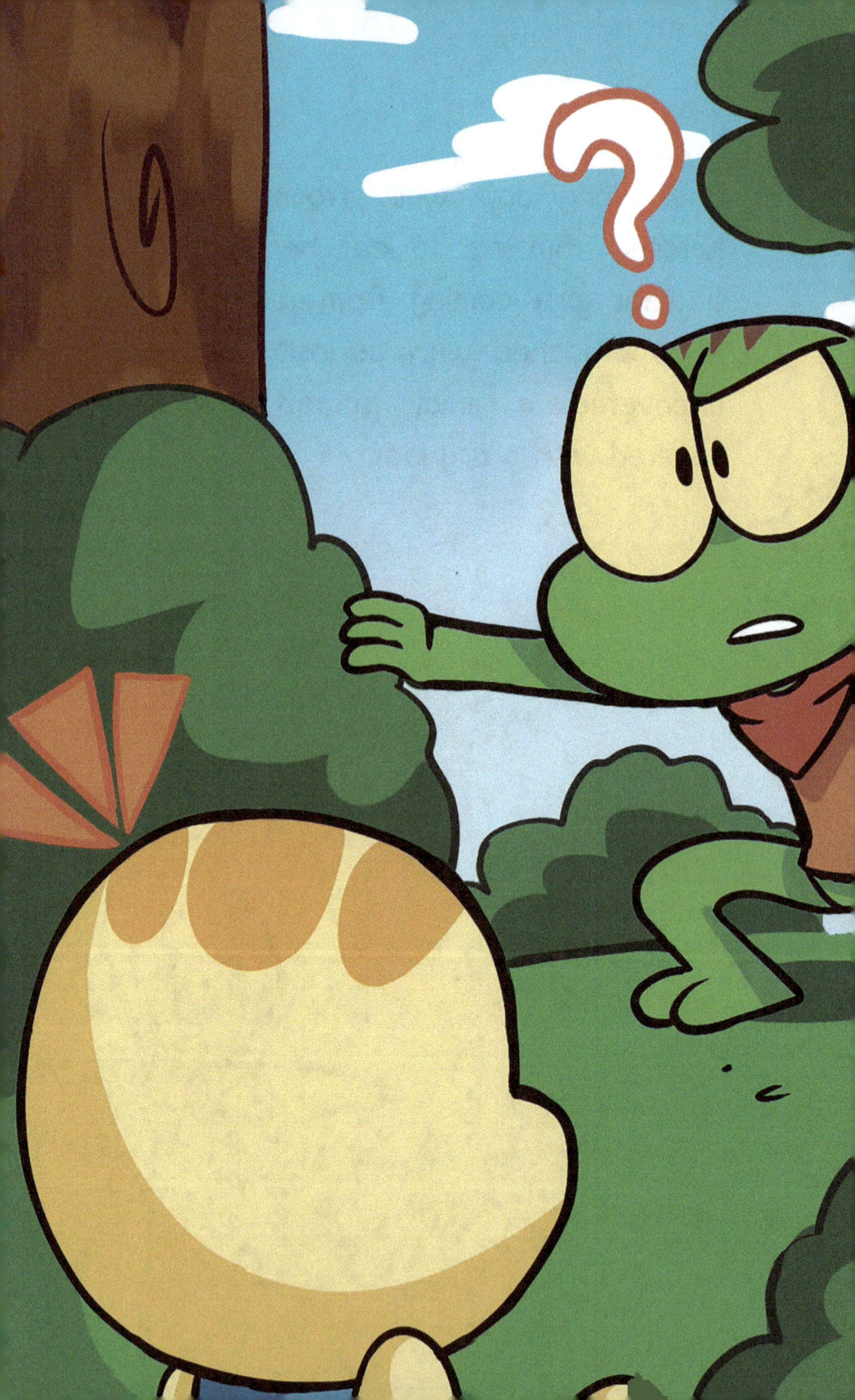

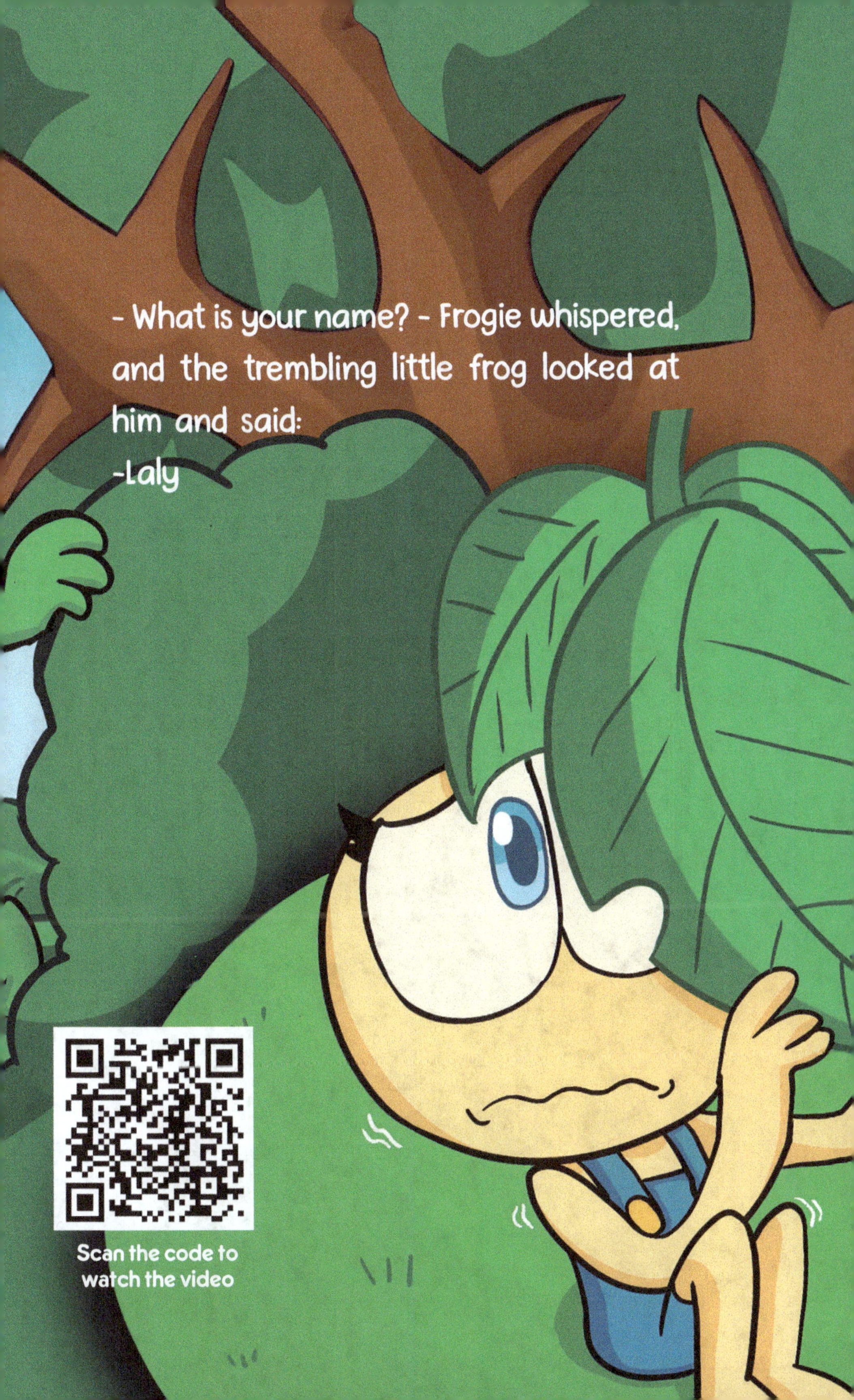

- What is your name? - Frogie whispered, and the trembling little frog looked at him and said:
-Laly
Scan the code to watch the video

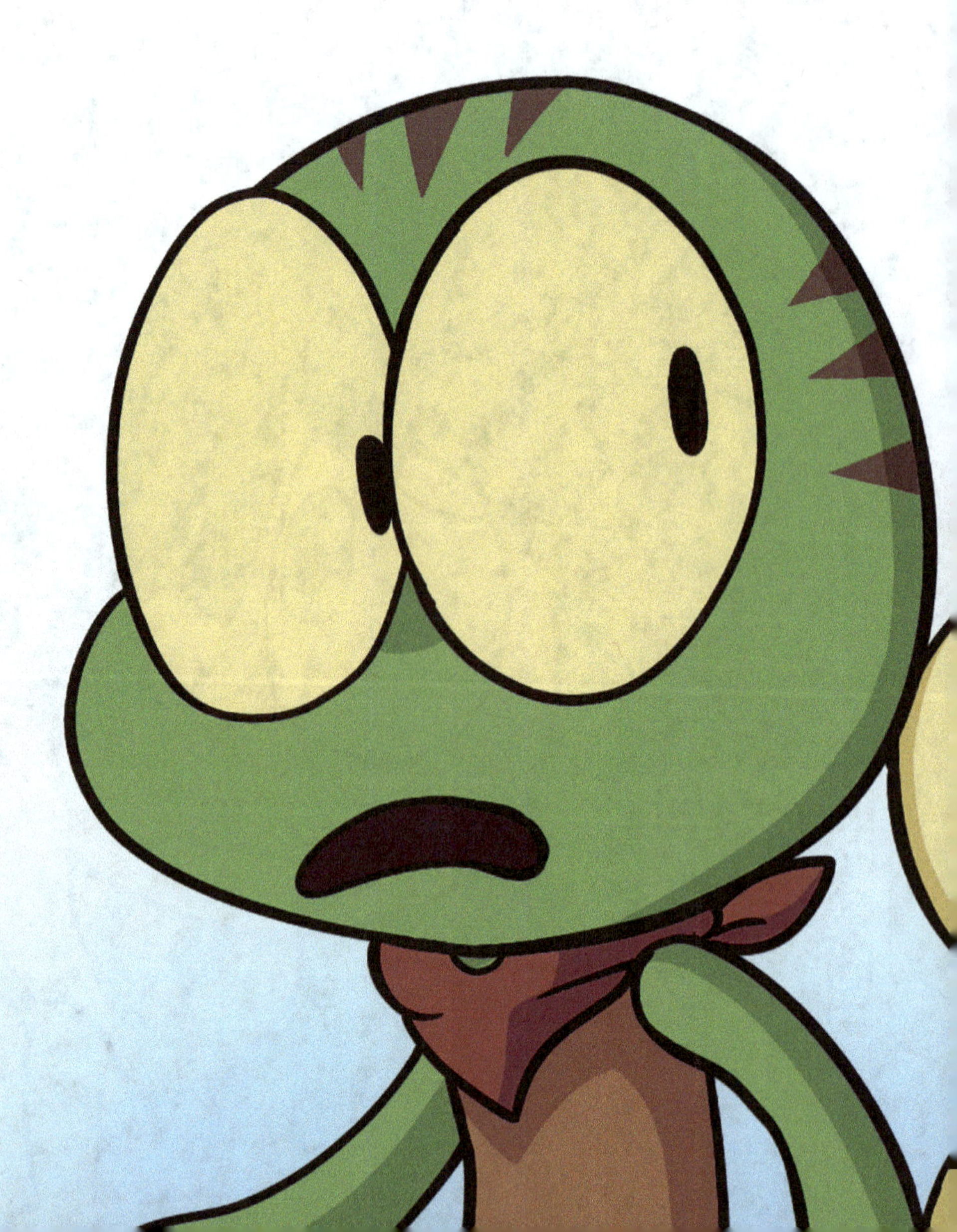

Instantly the howl of a coyote was heard. Frogie thought that it was surely Scar and without doubt he offered to help Laly escape from the feared beast.

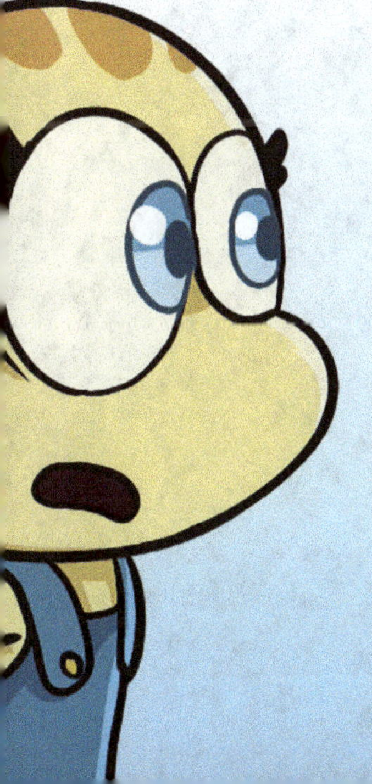

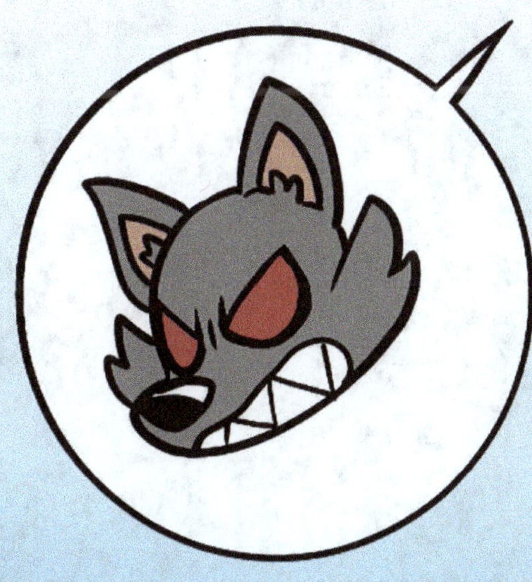

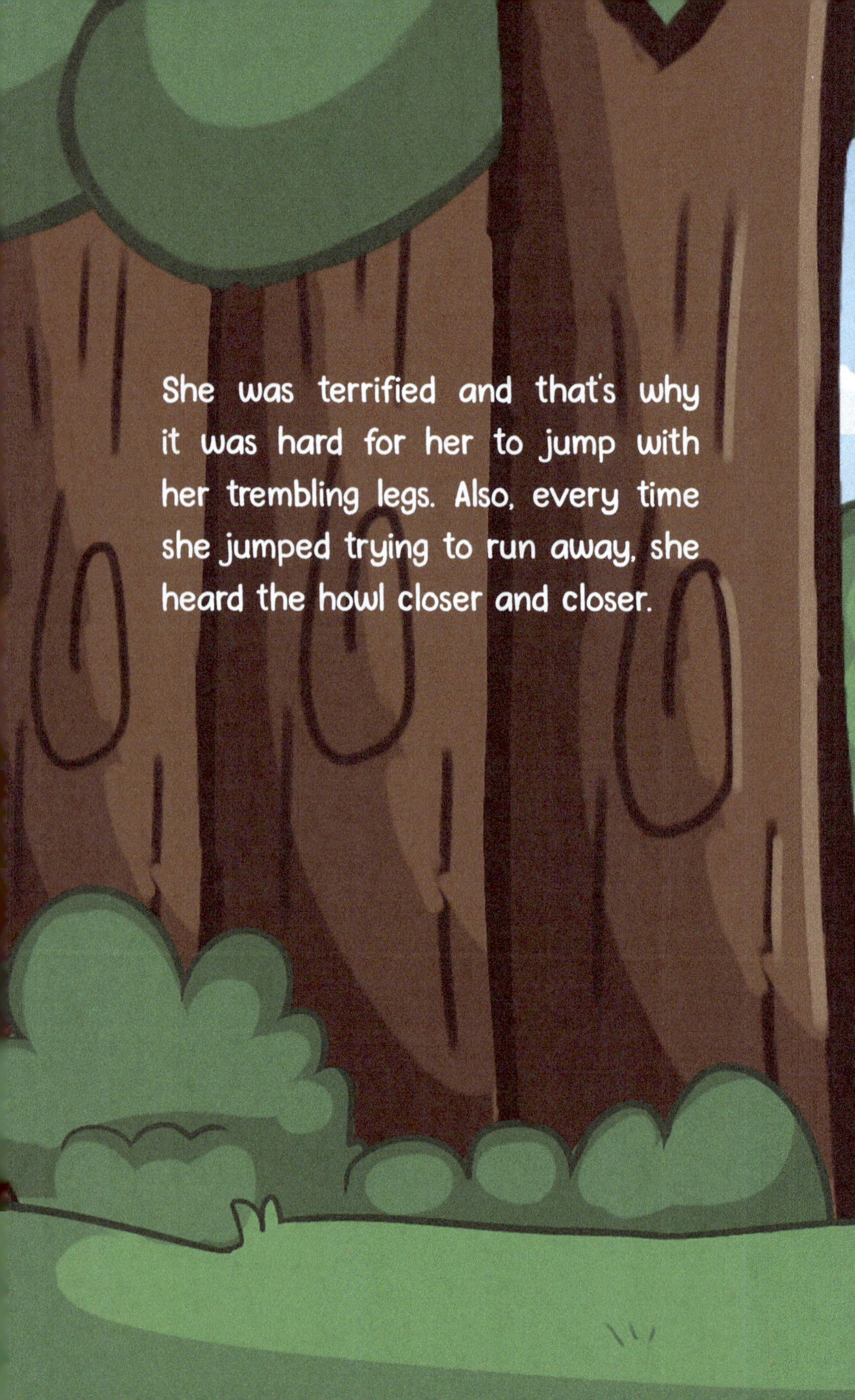

She was terrified and that's why it was hard for her to jump with her trembling legs. Also, every time she jumped trying to run away, she heard the howl closer and closer.

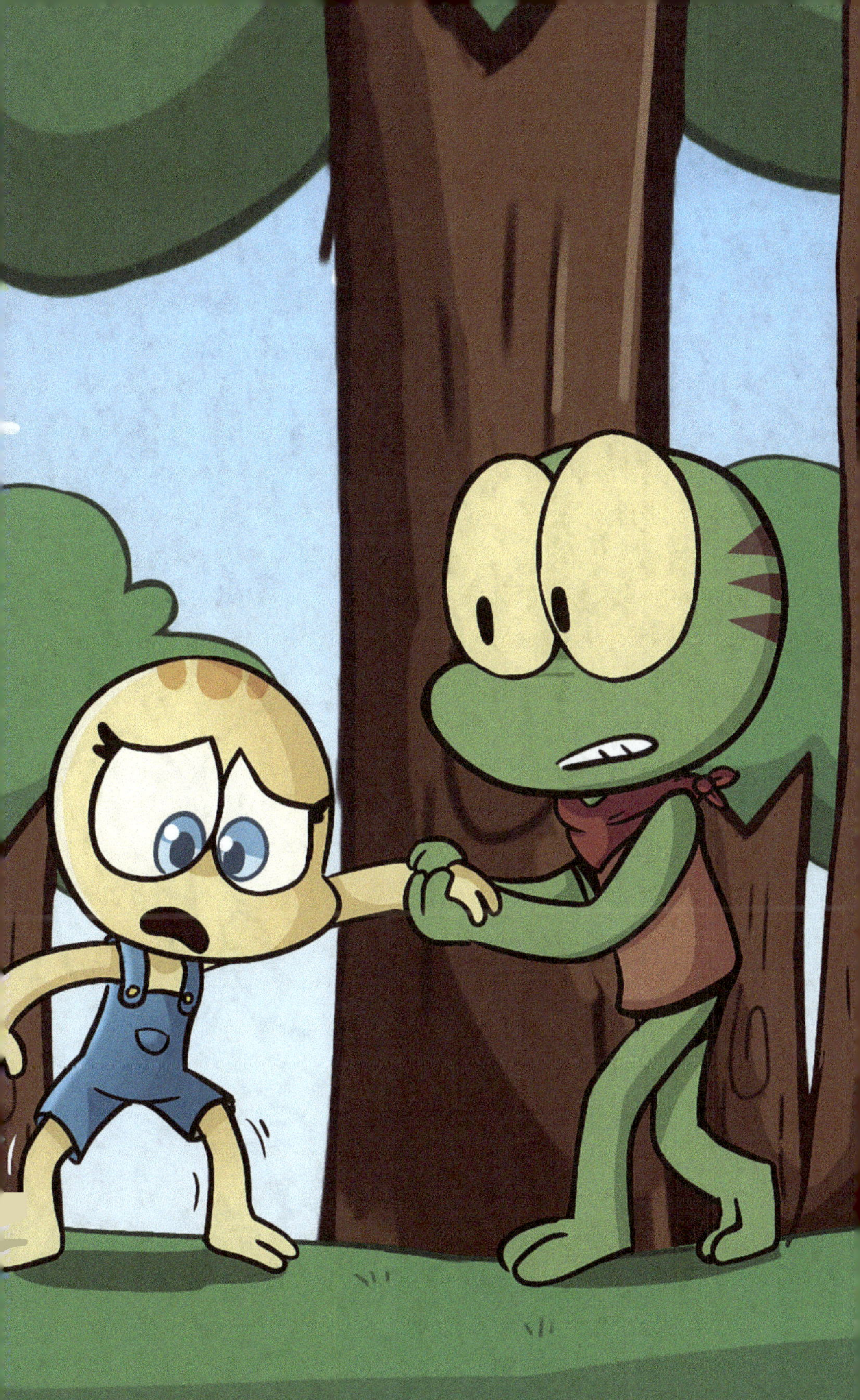

Frogie and Laly, seeing that they could not escape, together created a plan to face the coyote and protect the other habitants of Ranicor, so they decided to build a trap and attract Scar into it.

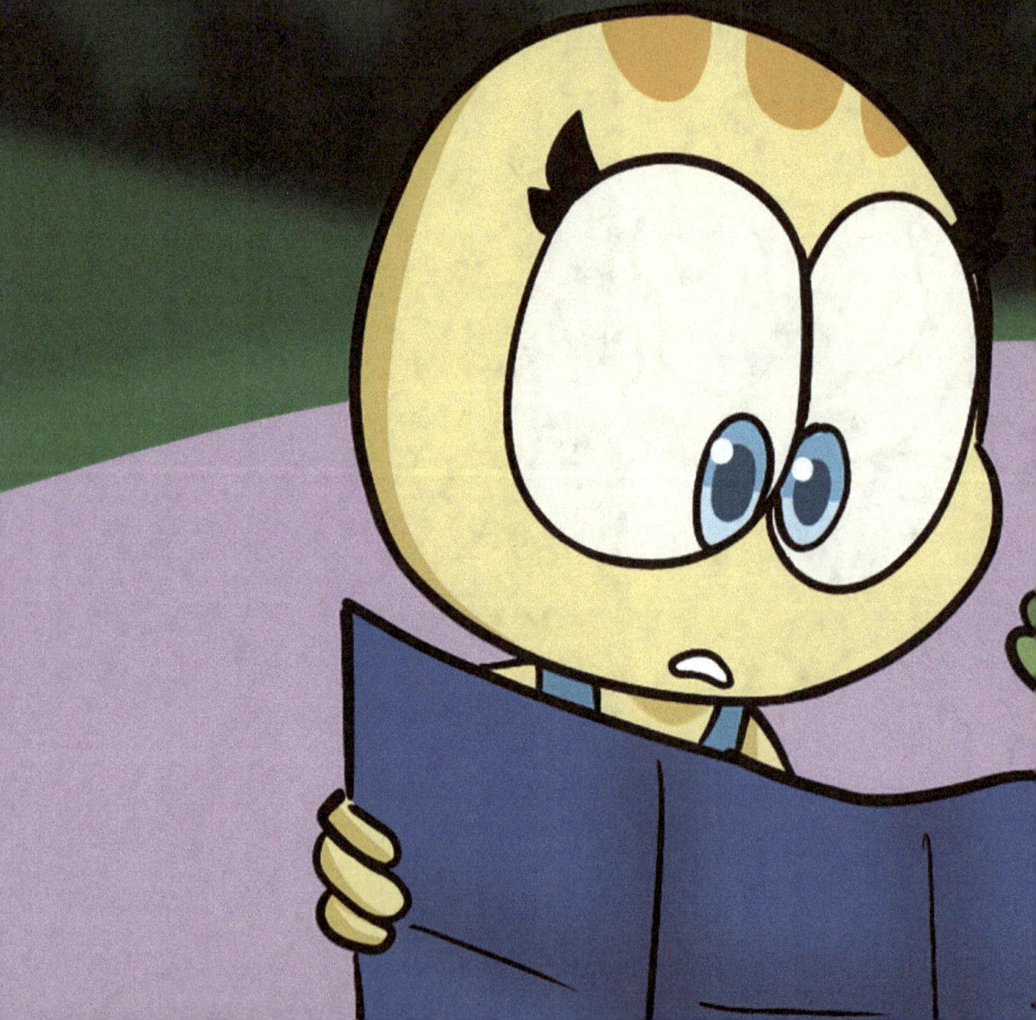

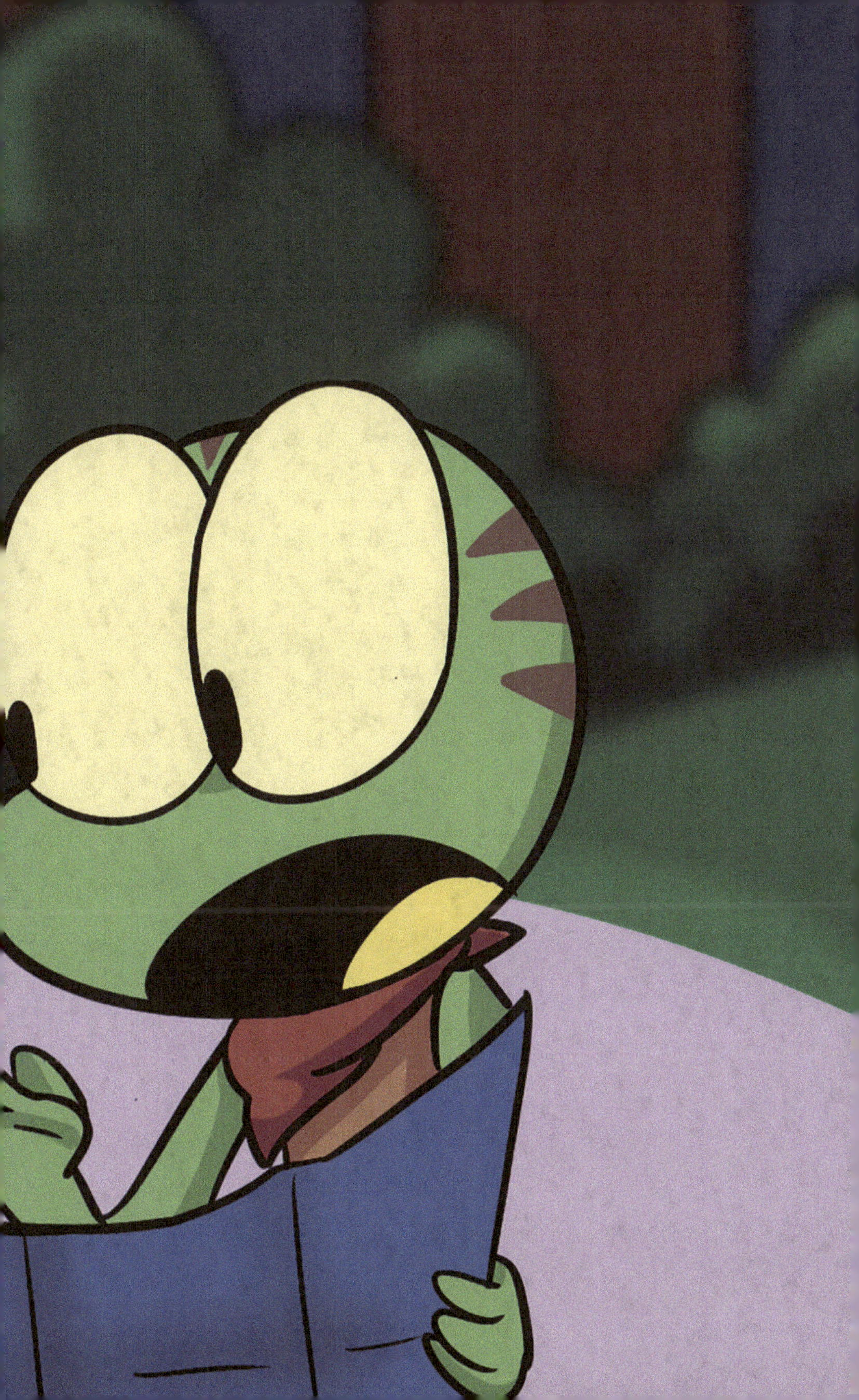

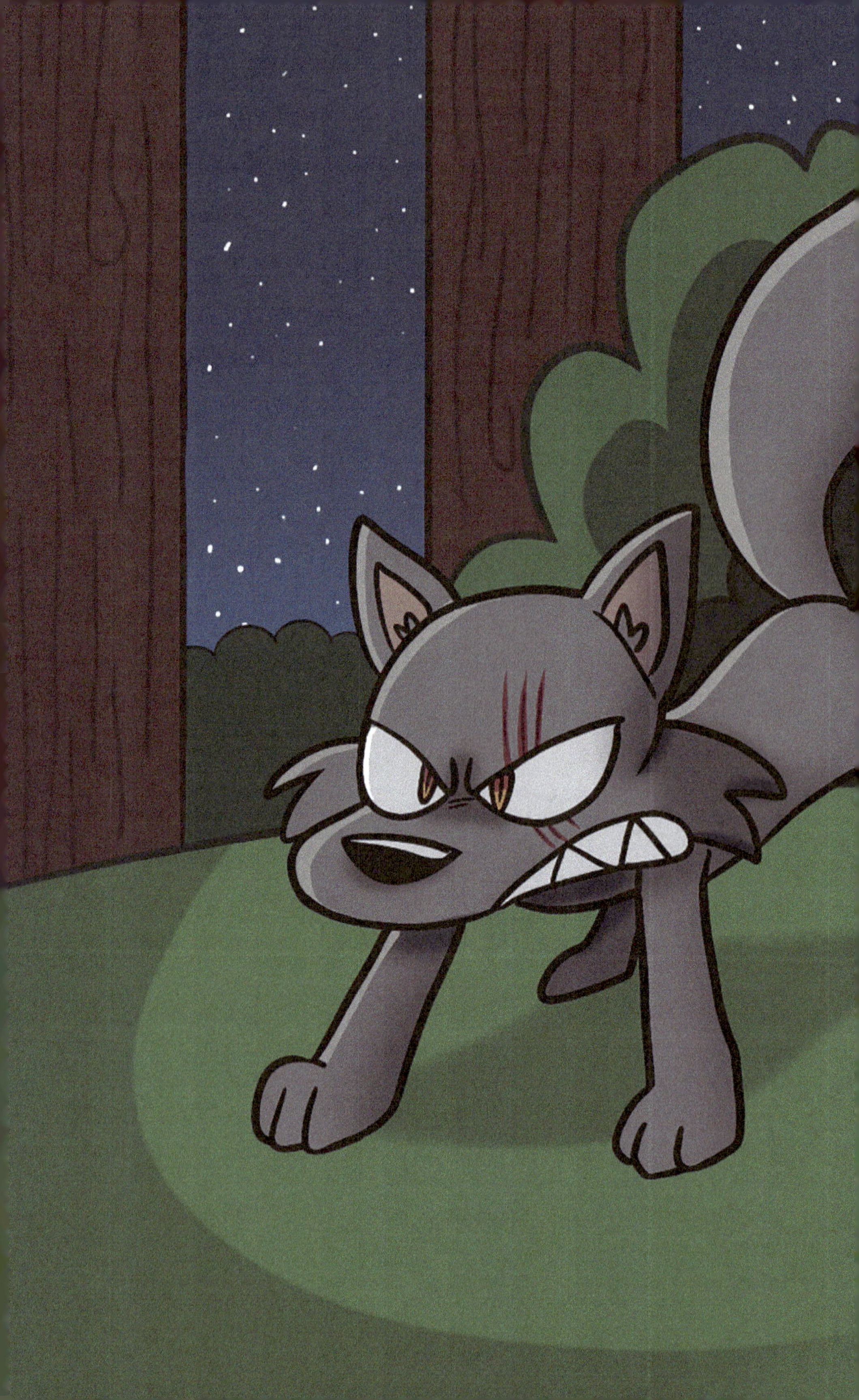

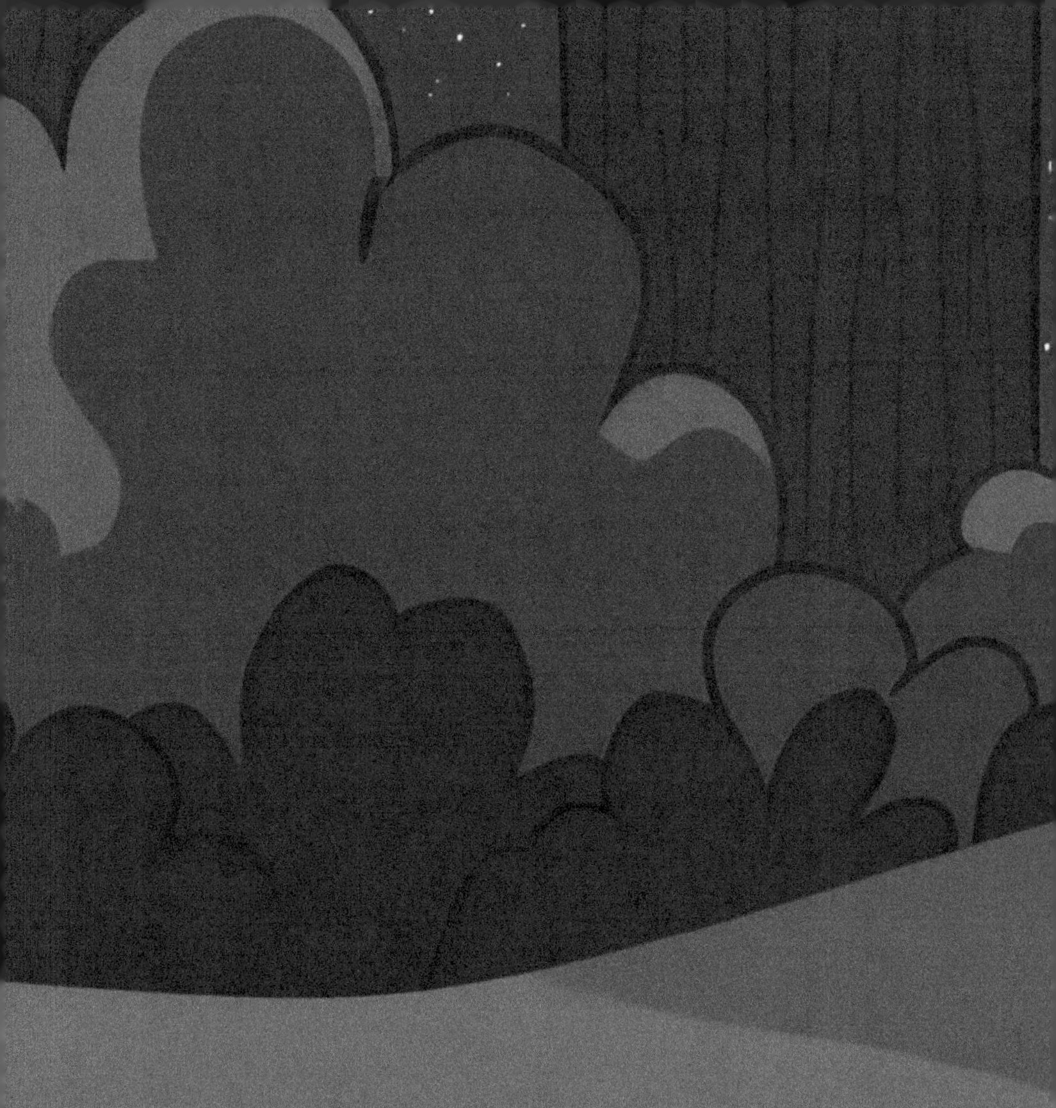

Night fell and the malignant presence of the fearsome coyote with the scar on its right eye was felt.

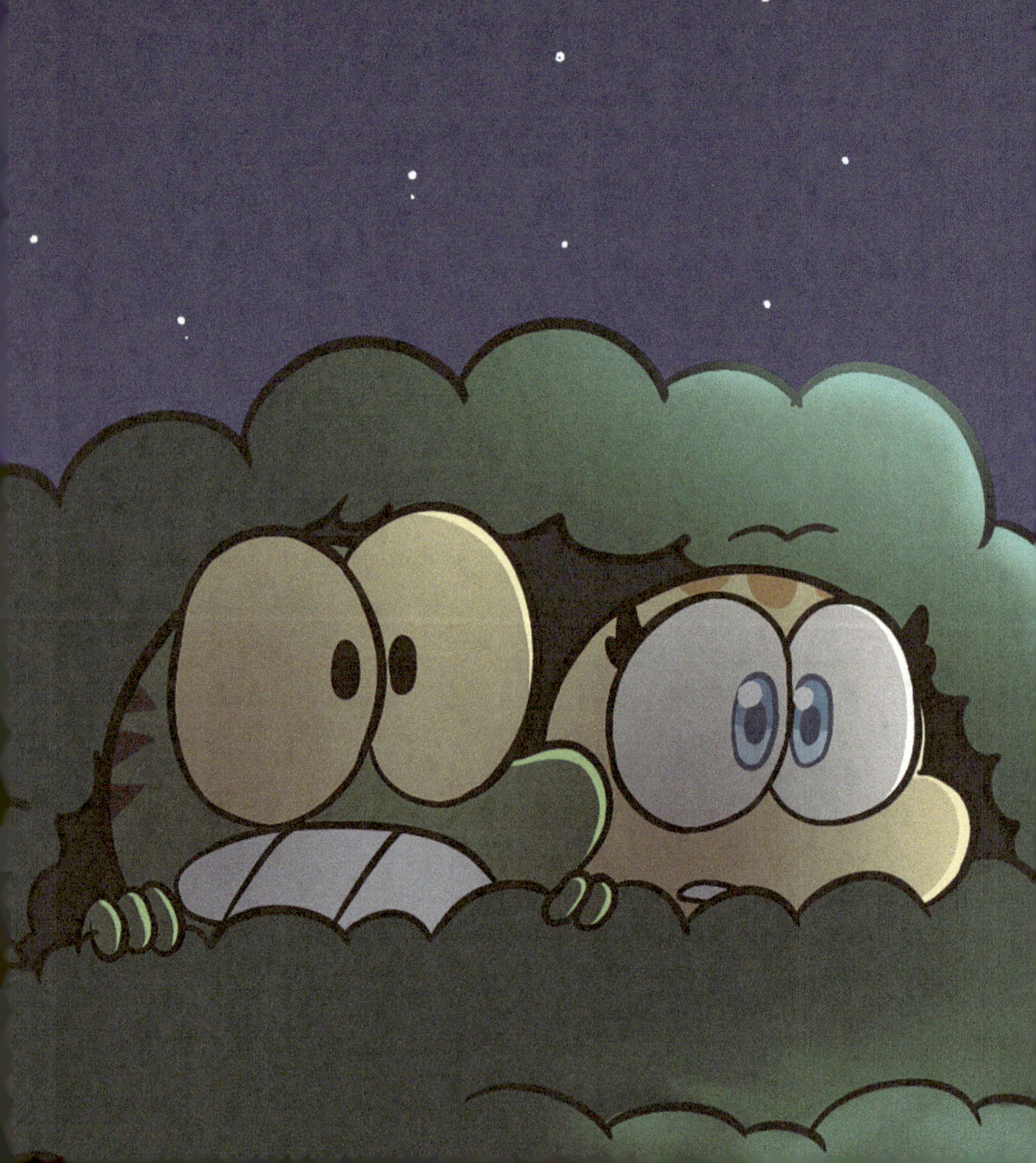

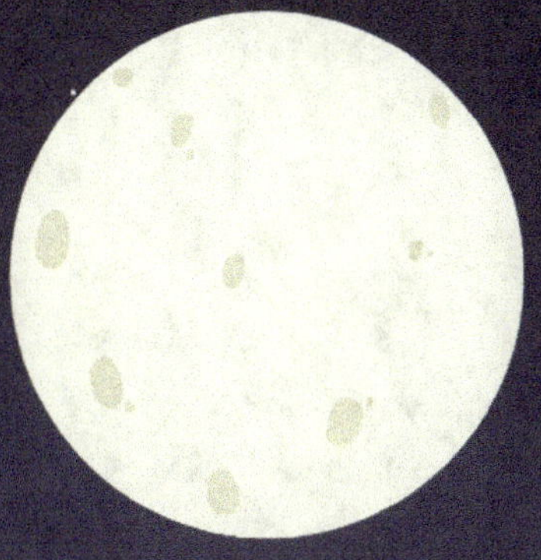

Frogie and Laly hid behind some bushes and waited patiently for Scar to appear and fall in the trap,

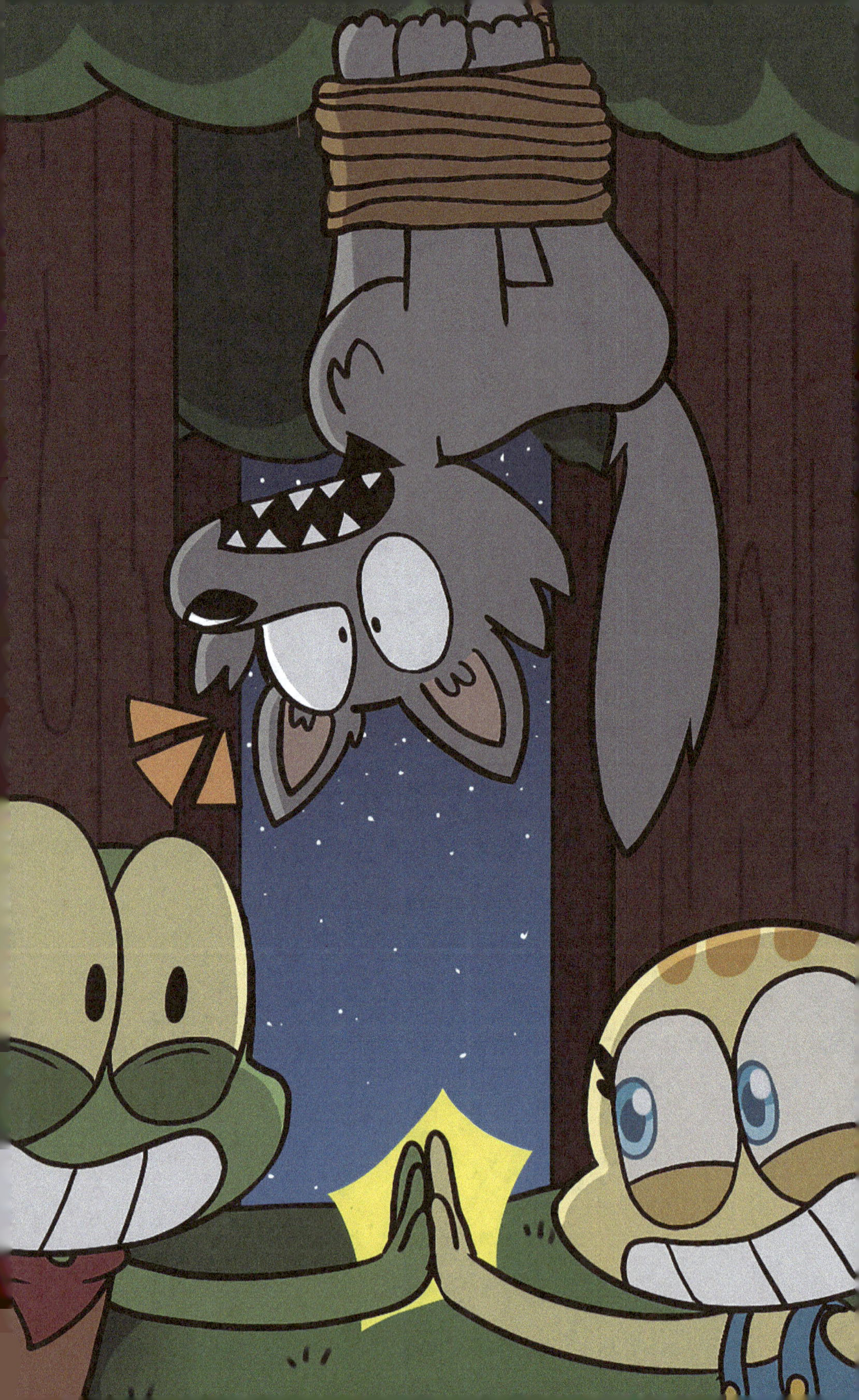

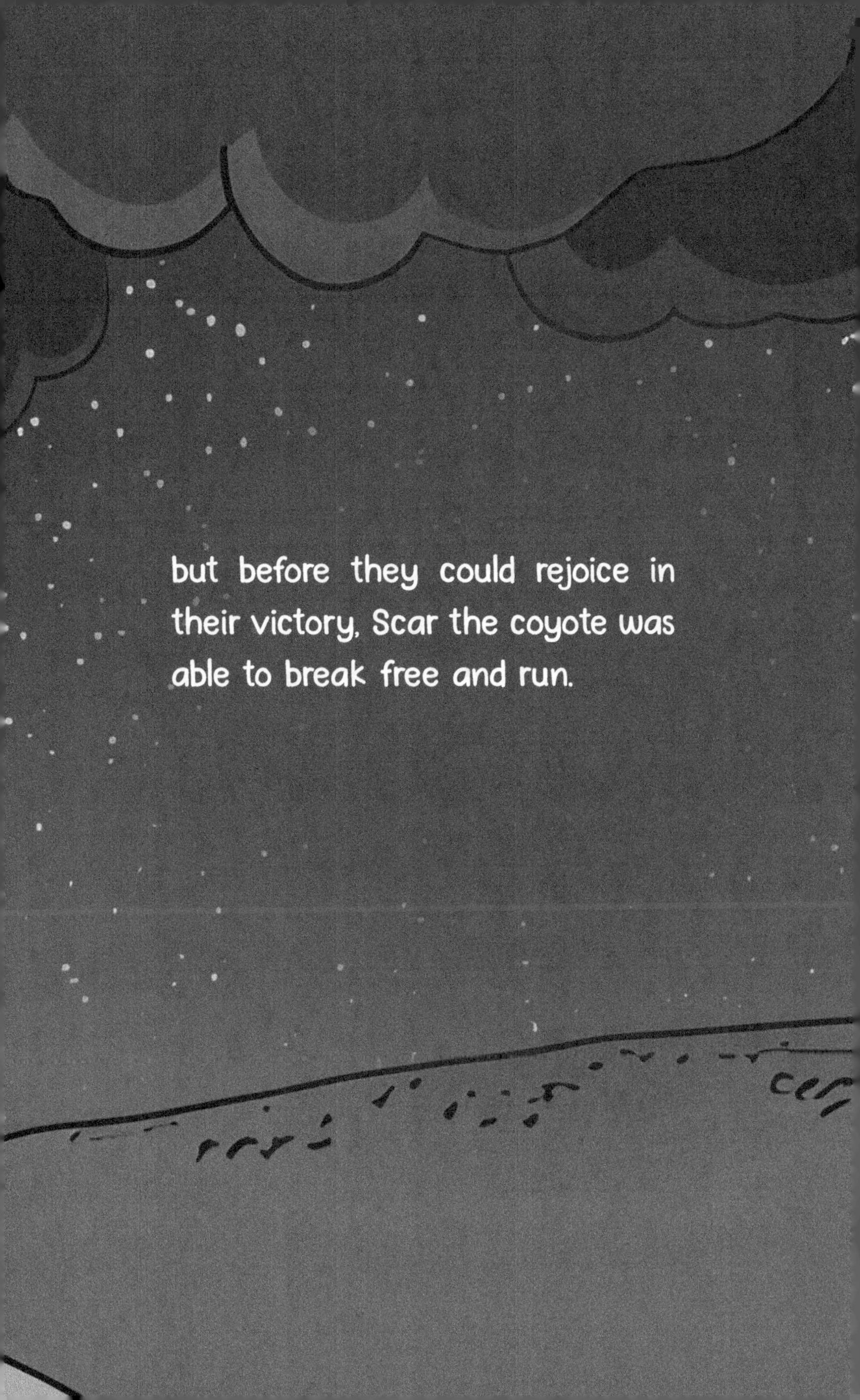

but before they could rejoice in
their victory, Scar the coyote was
able to break free and run.

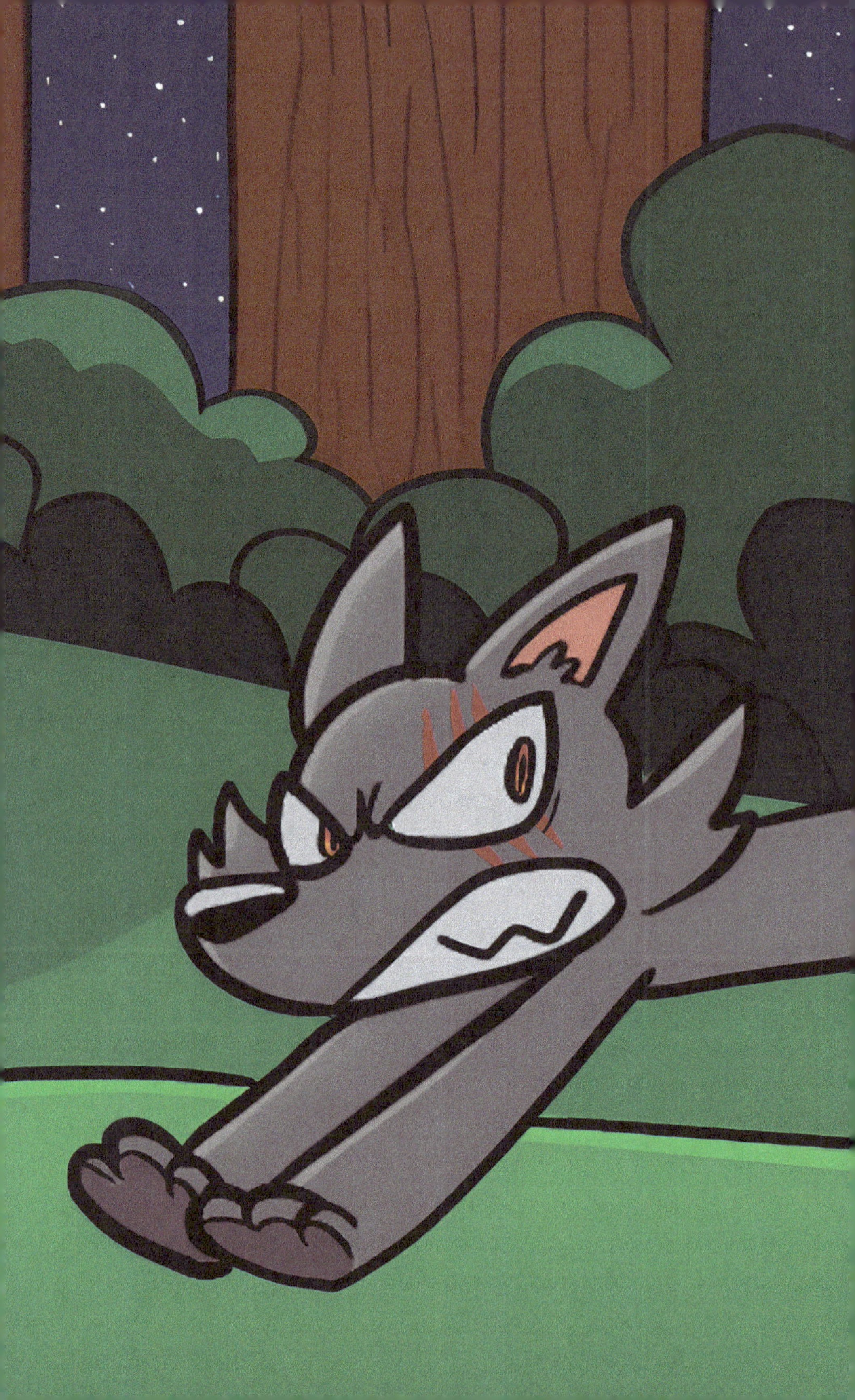

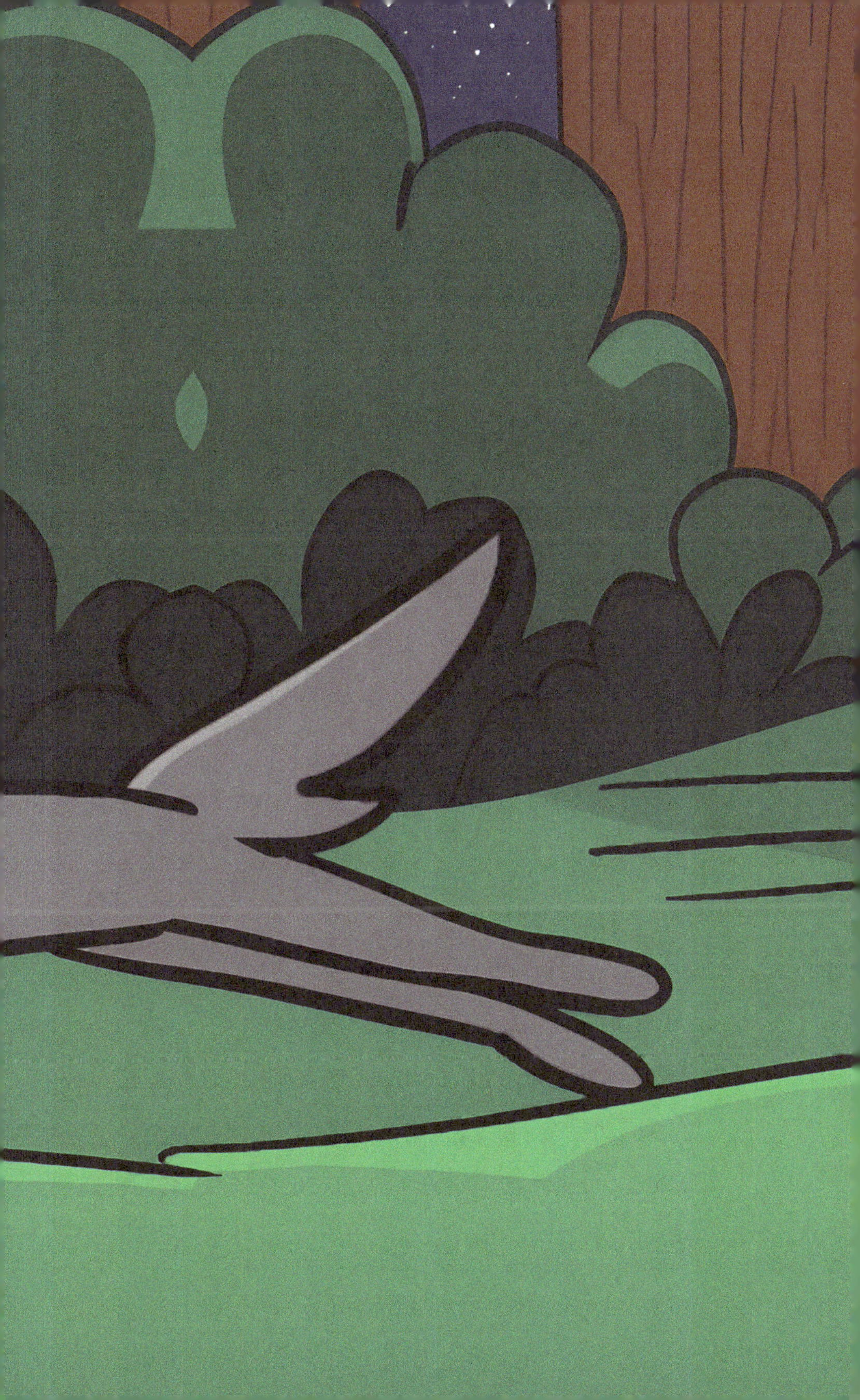

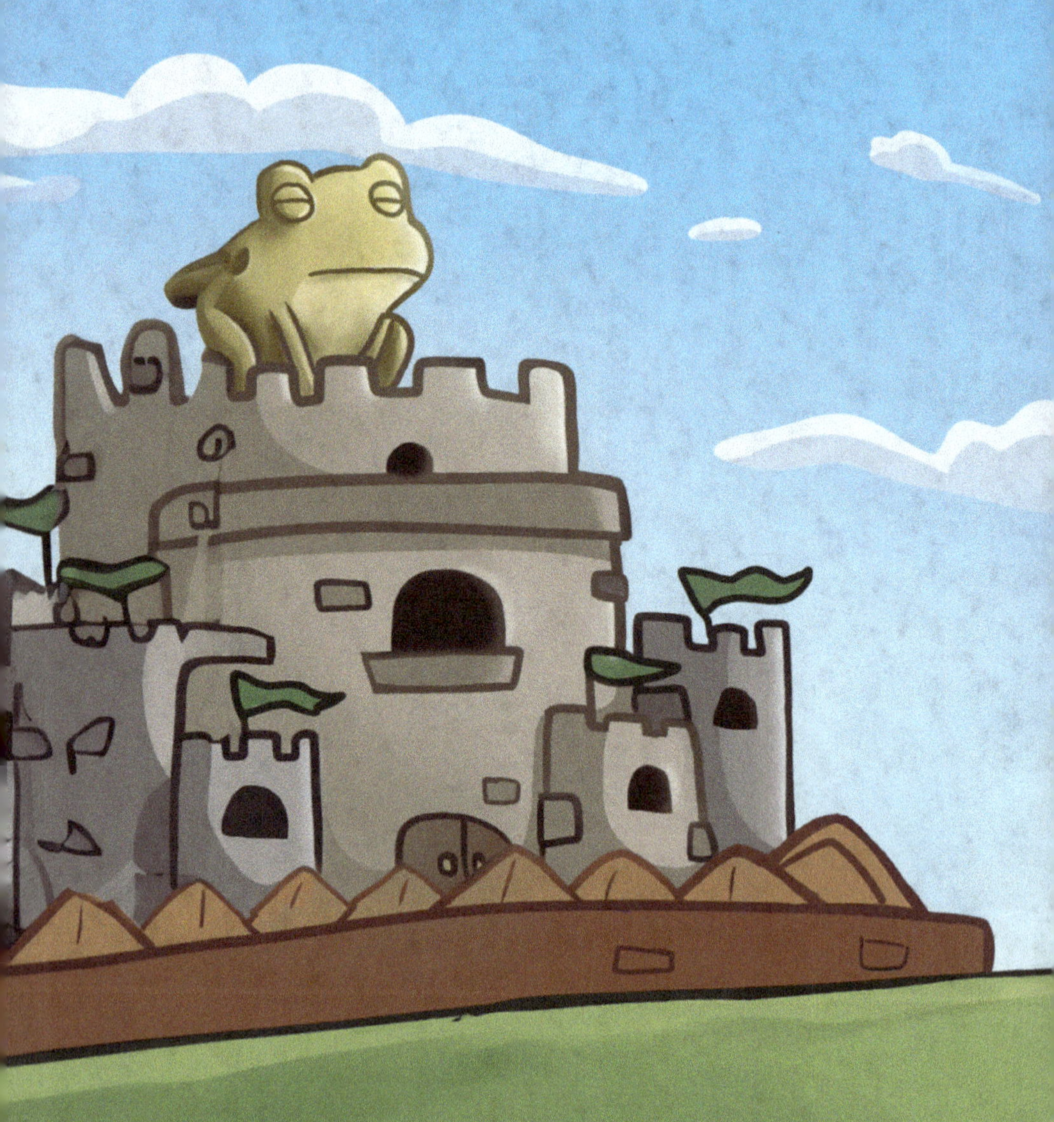

After that frightening adventure, Frogie
and Laly grew closer until they became
good friends. They knew that Scar

had fled, but it seemed that he had decided not to attack the kingdom, perhaps out of fear to fall into a trap once again.

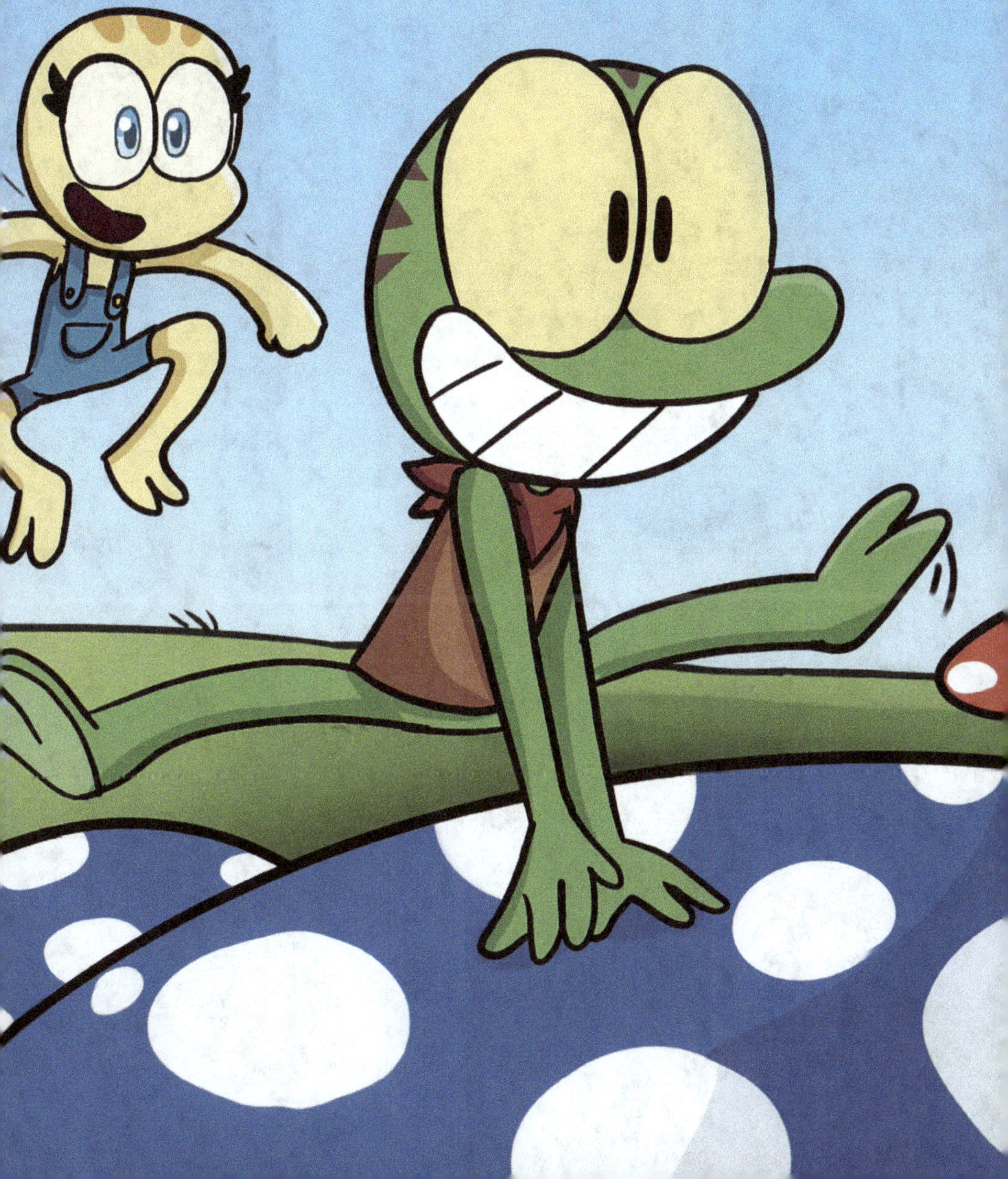

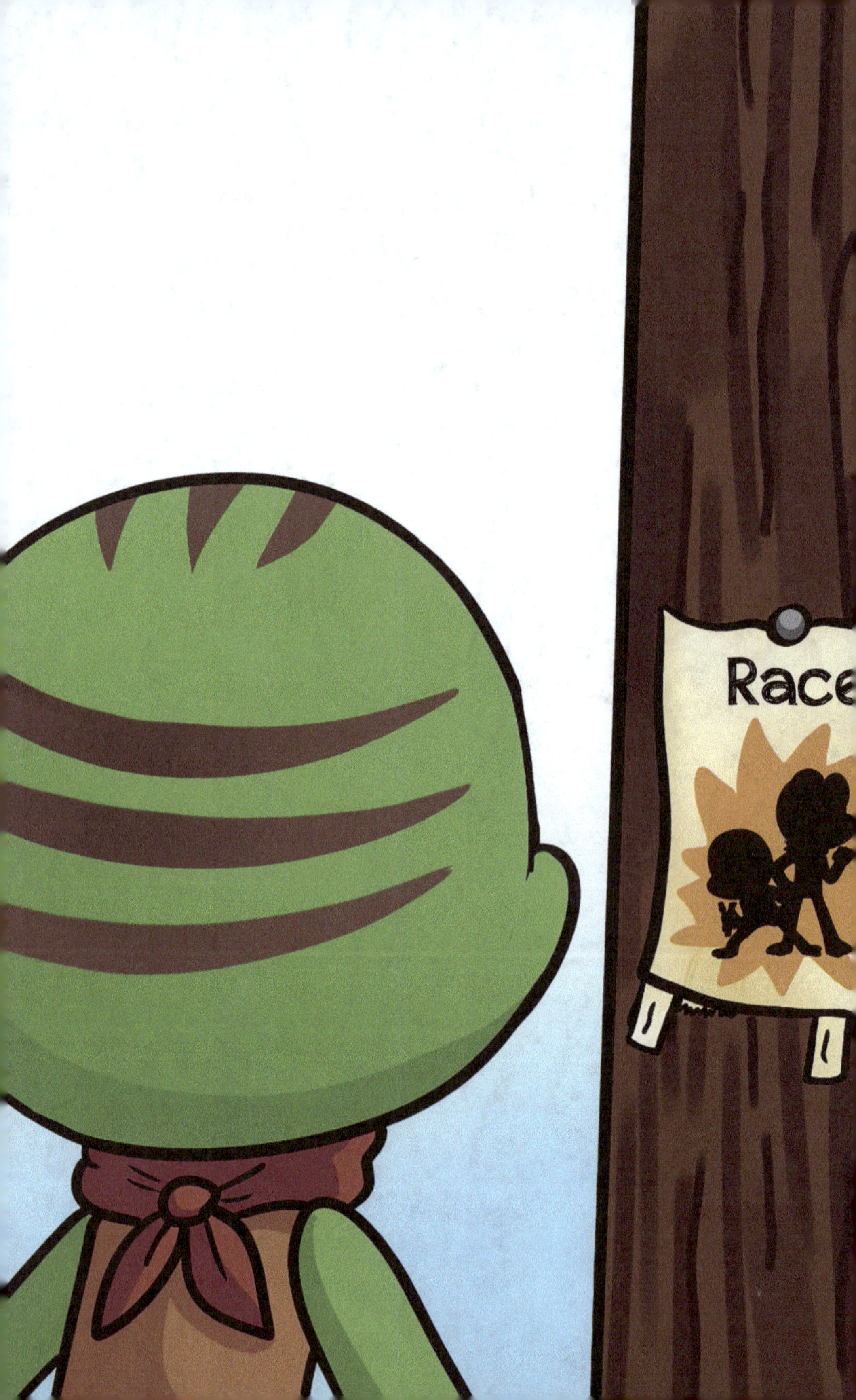
Race

The following summer, they found out that the king had organized an obstacle run to commemorate Ranicor's centenary; and they decided to participate as a team.

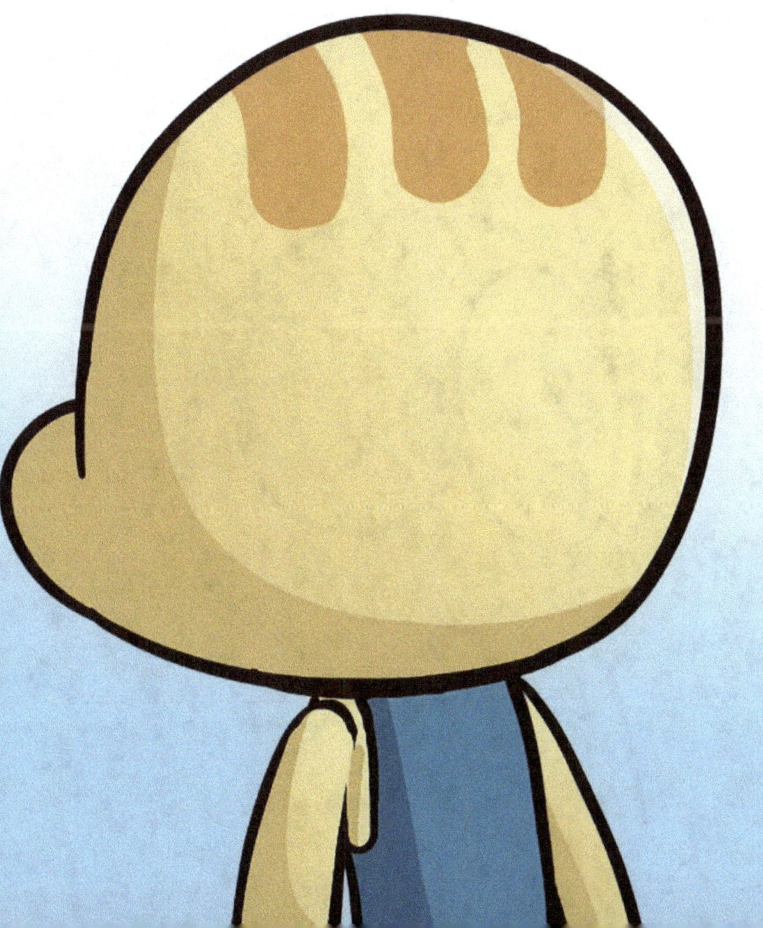

When the big test came, Frogie knew it was his chance to prove his loyalty, bravery, and strength.

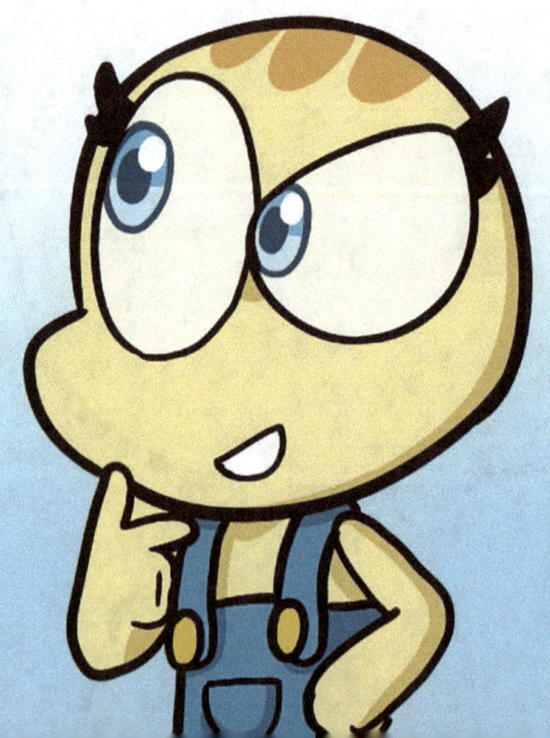

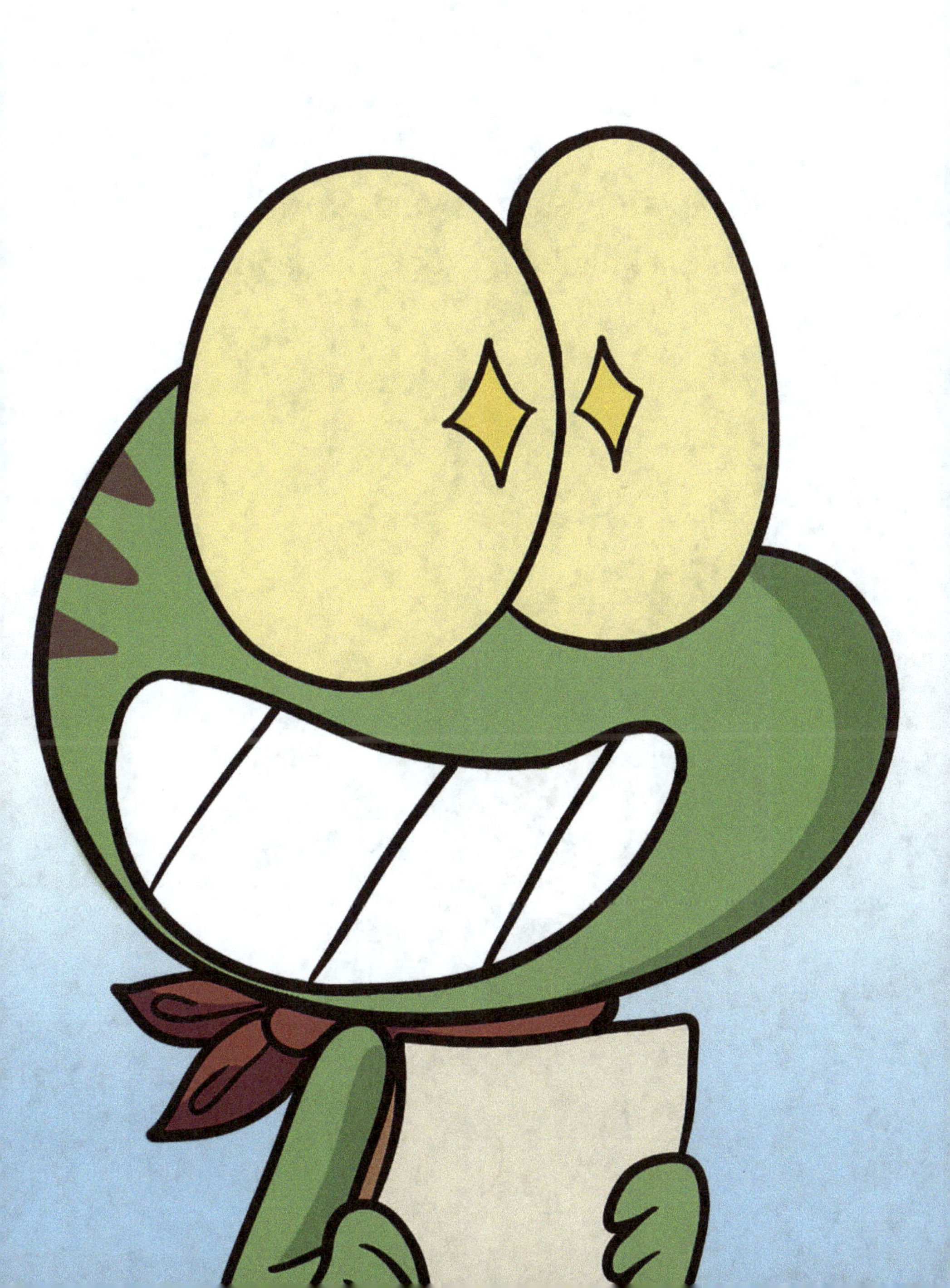

The race started and Frogie and
Laly immediately took the lead.

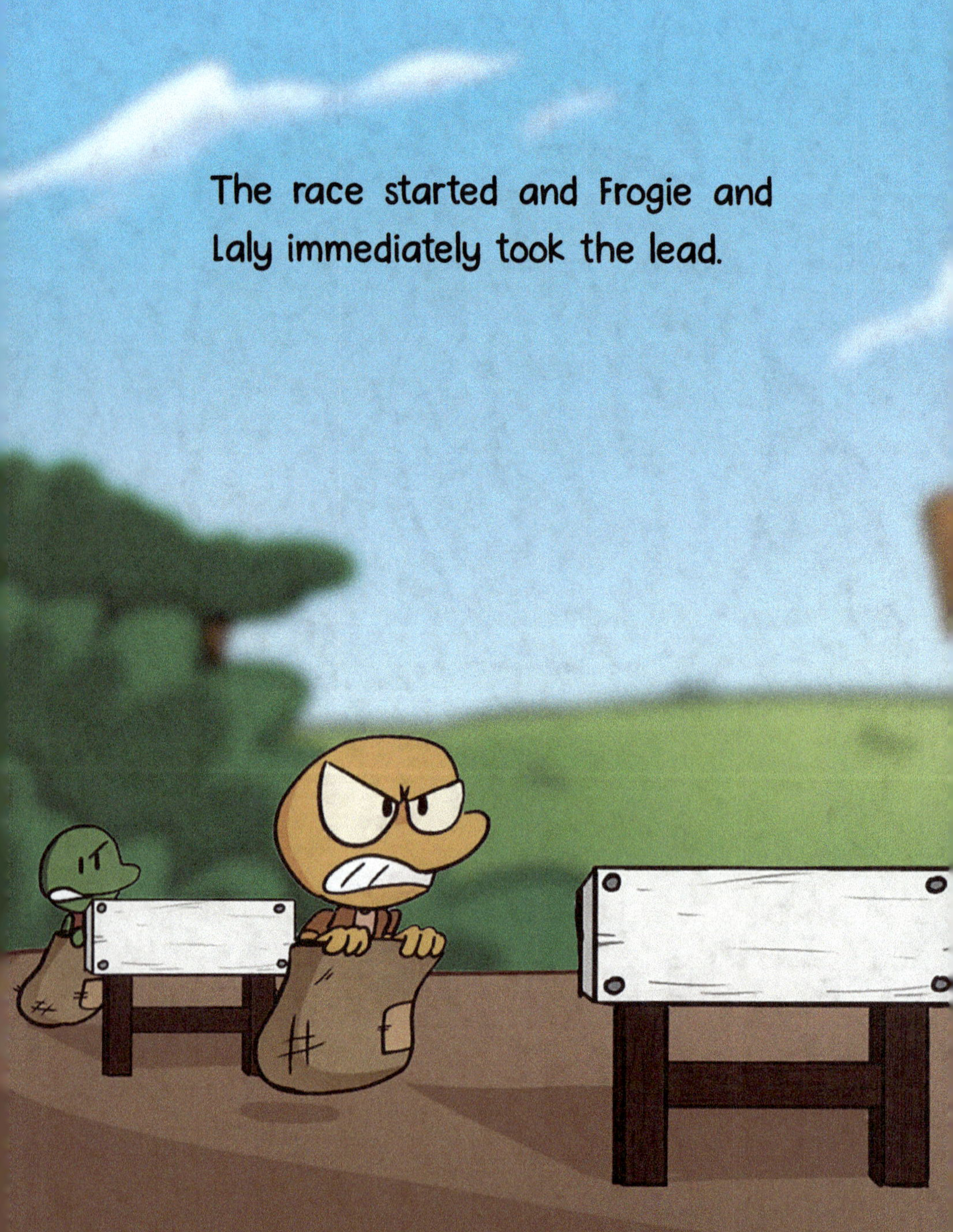

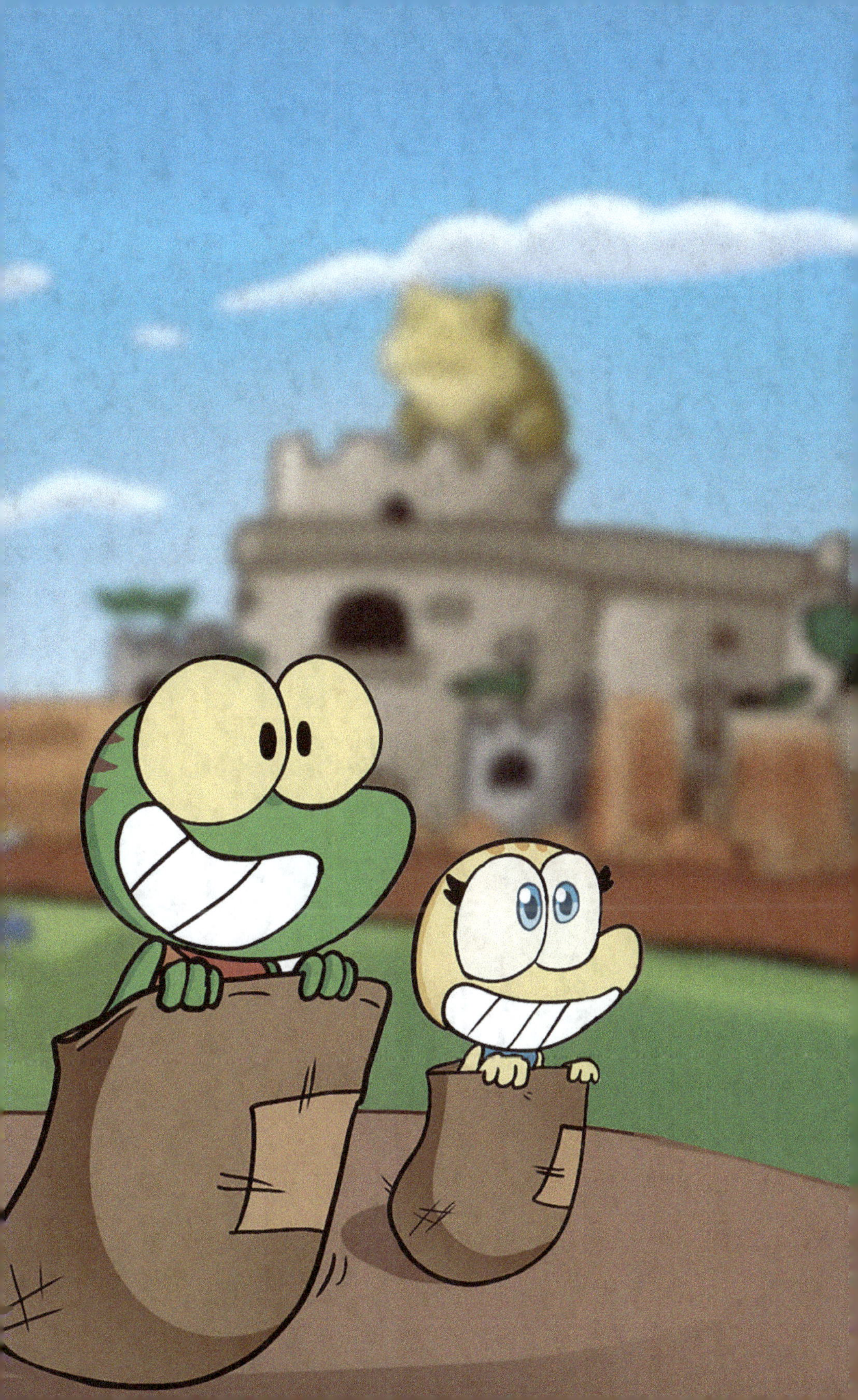

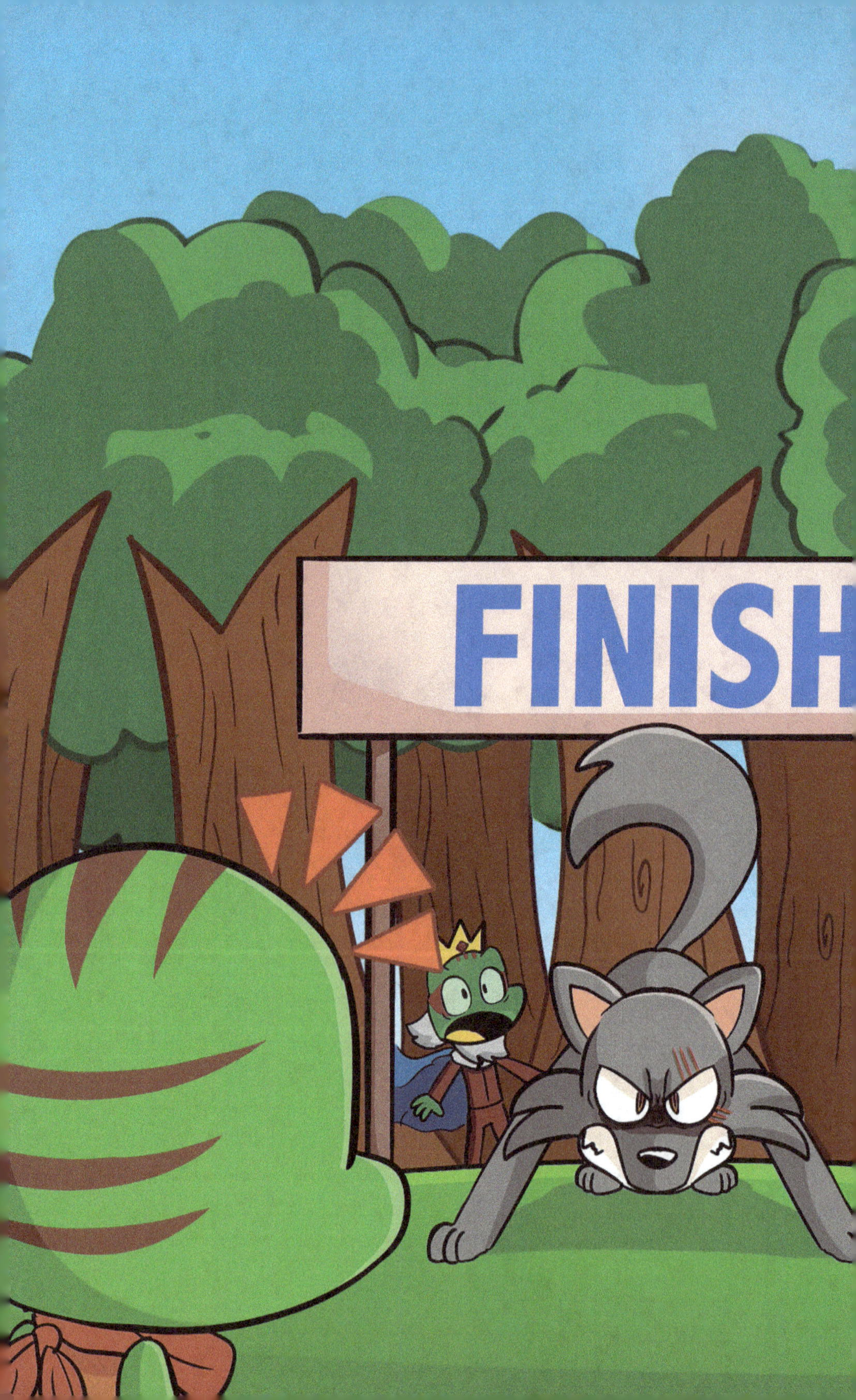

FINISH

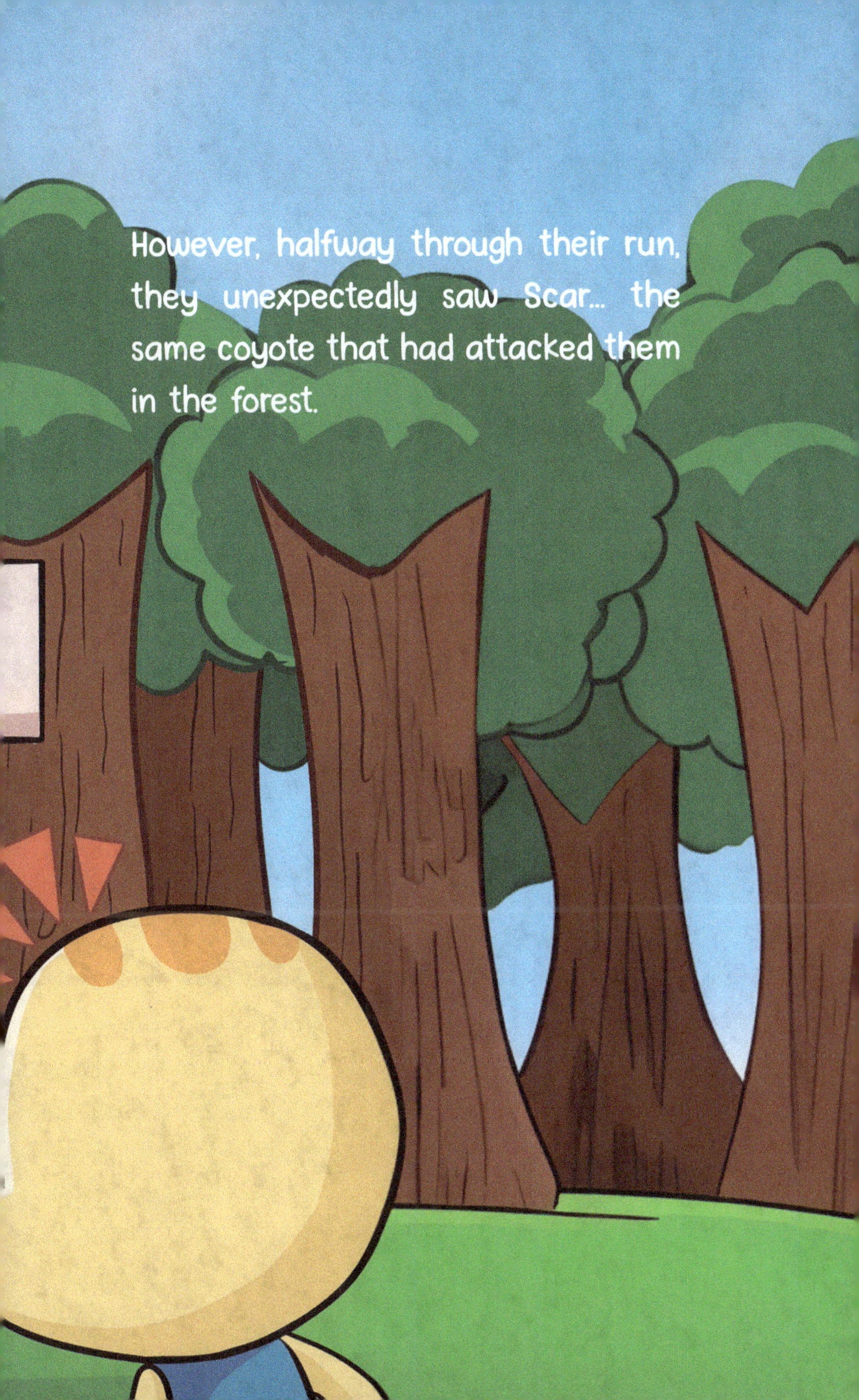

However, halfway through their run, they unexpectedly saw Scar... the same coyote that had attacked them in the forest.

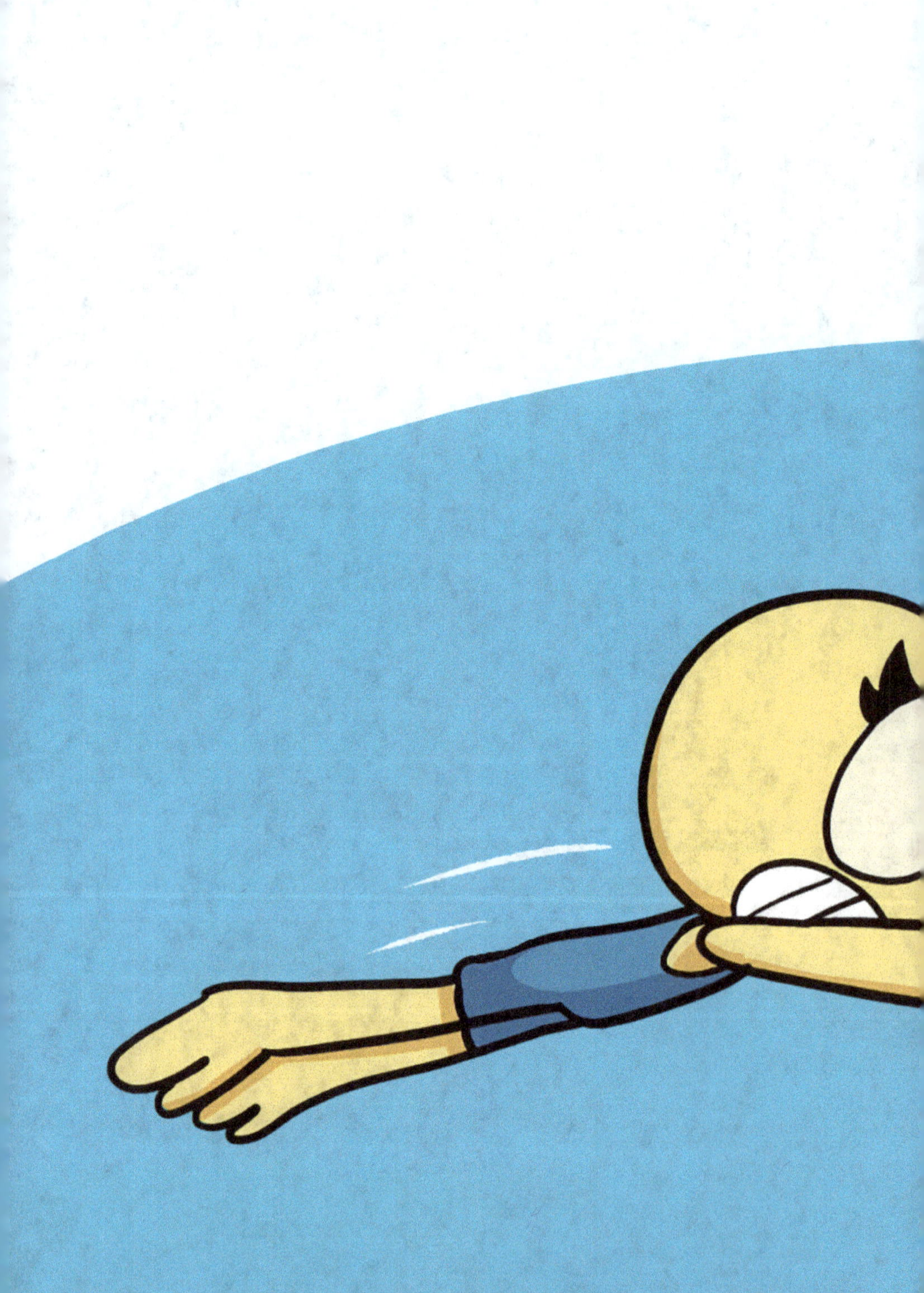

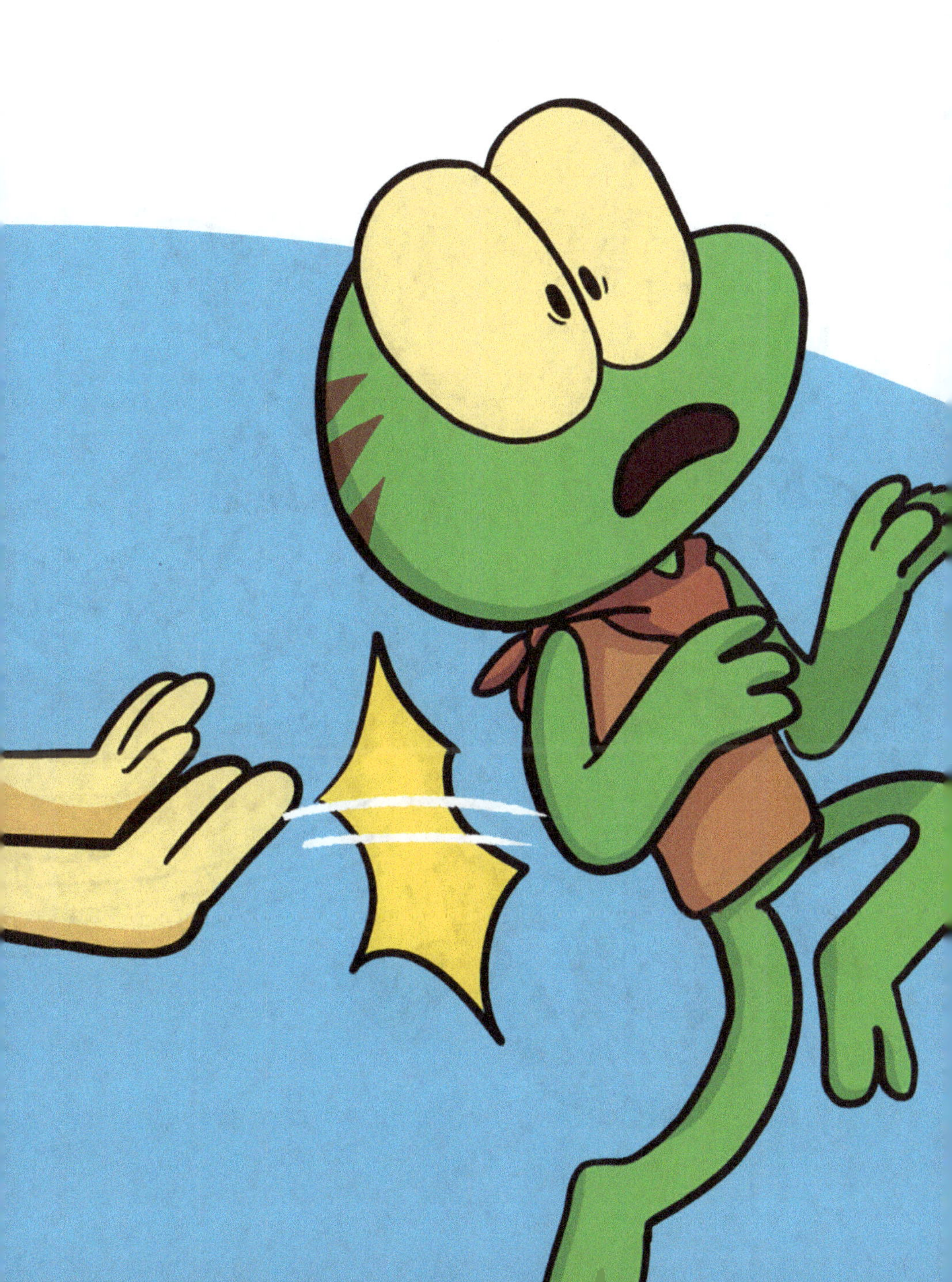

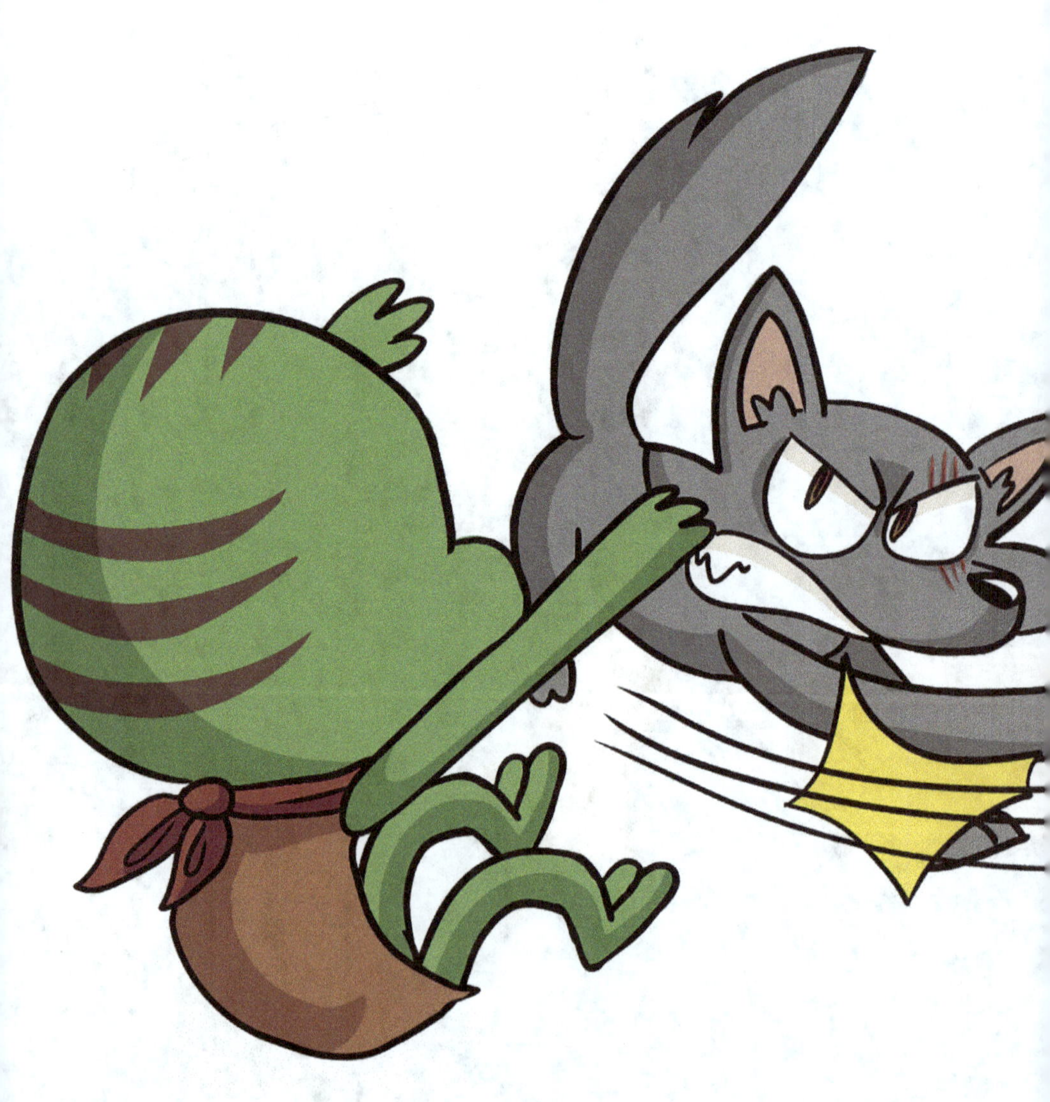

He tried to attack Frogie, but when Laly saw him moving so fast and violently, she tried to save her friend. That's when Scar hit her, knocking her unconscious.

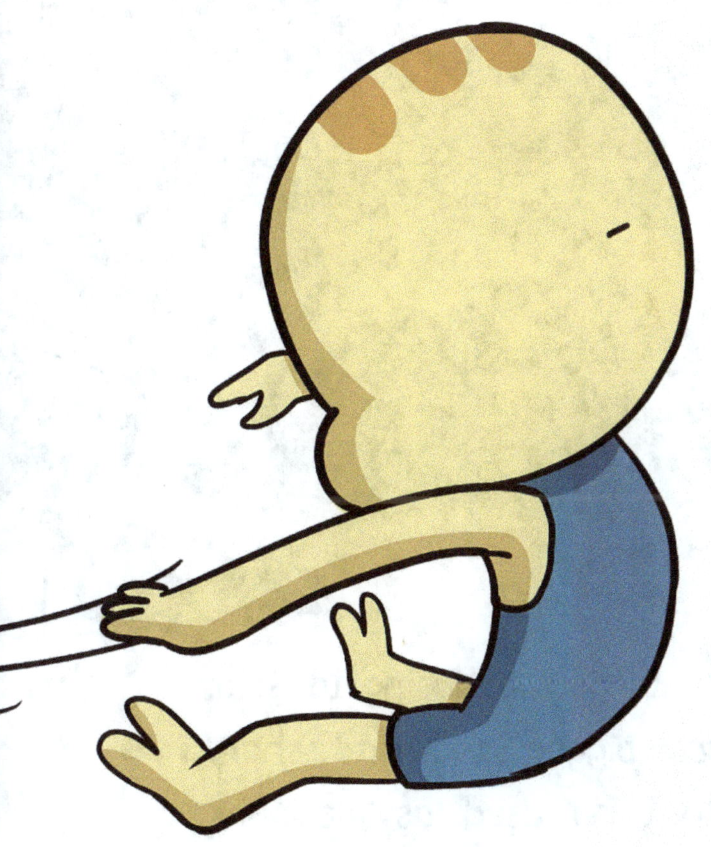

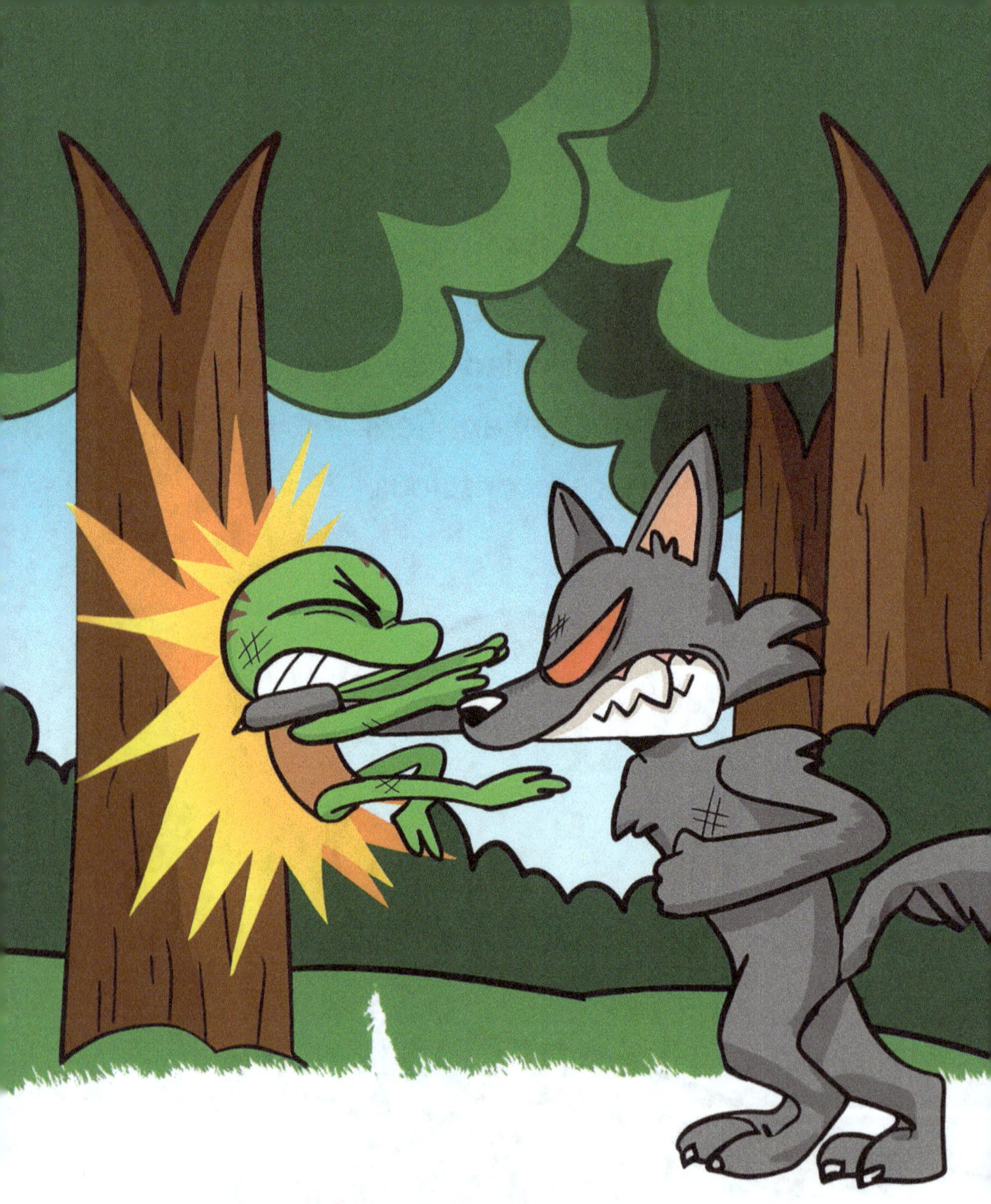

Frogie knew he was losing to Scar, who was bigger and had sharp fangs that he used as weapons, but he refused to give up. He made the decision to fight the coyote and teach him a lesson, because he couldn't allow him to continue terrorizing the residents of Ranicor or, worse still, harming his friend Laly.

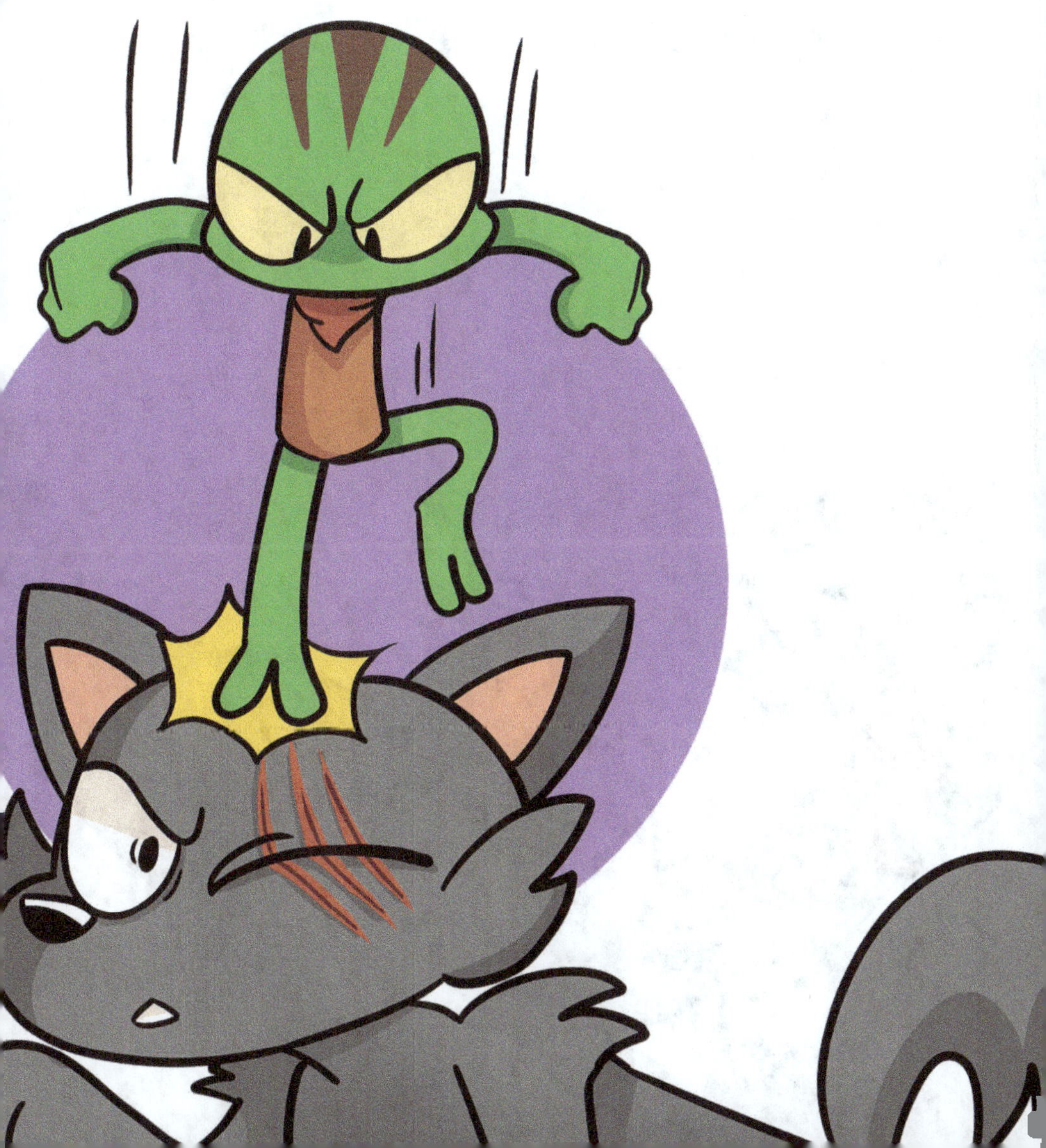

Because of this, Froggy fought with all his might, proving to be a brave and skilled fighter. He deflected the coyote's blows and kicked and punched him to make him back up.

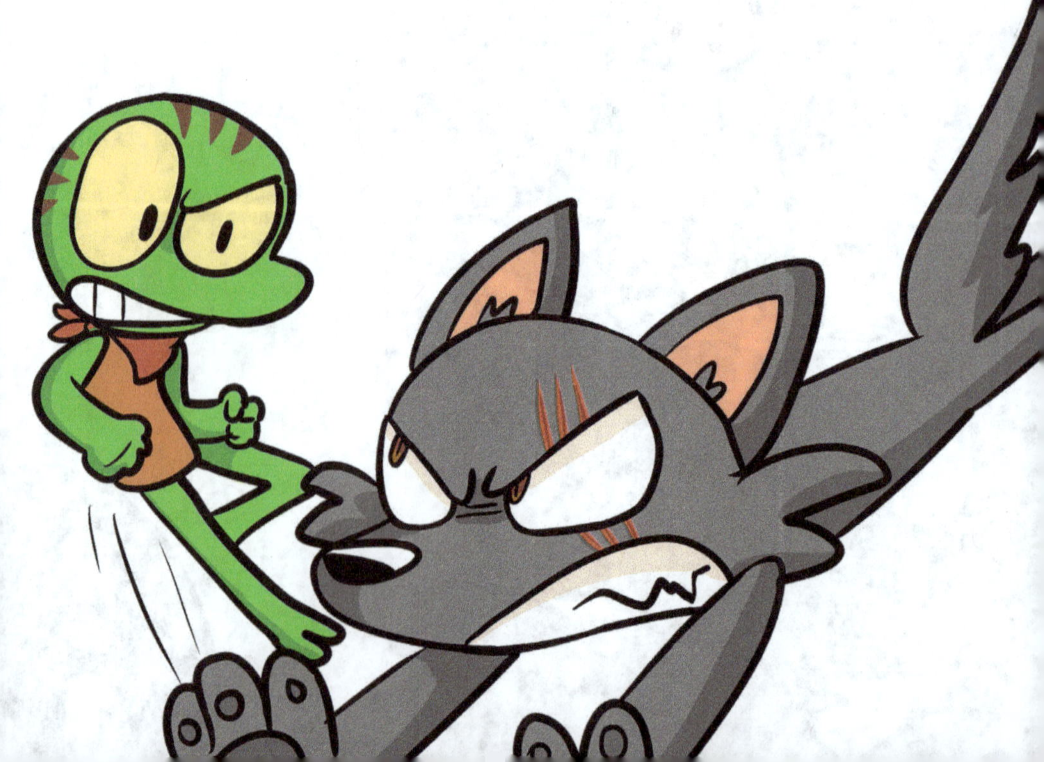

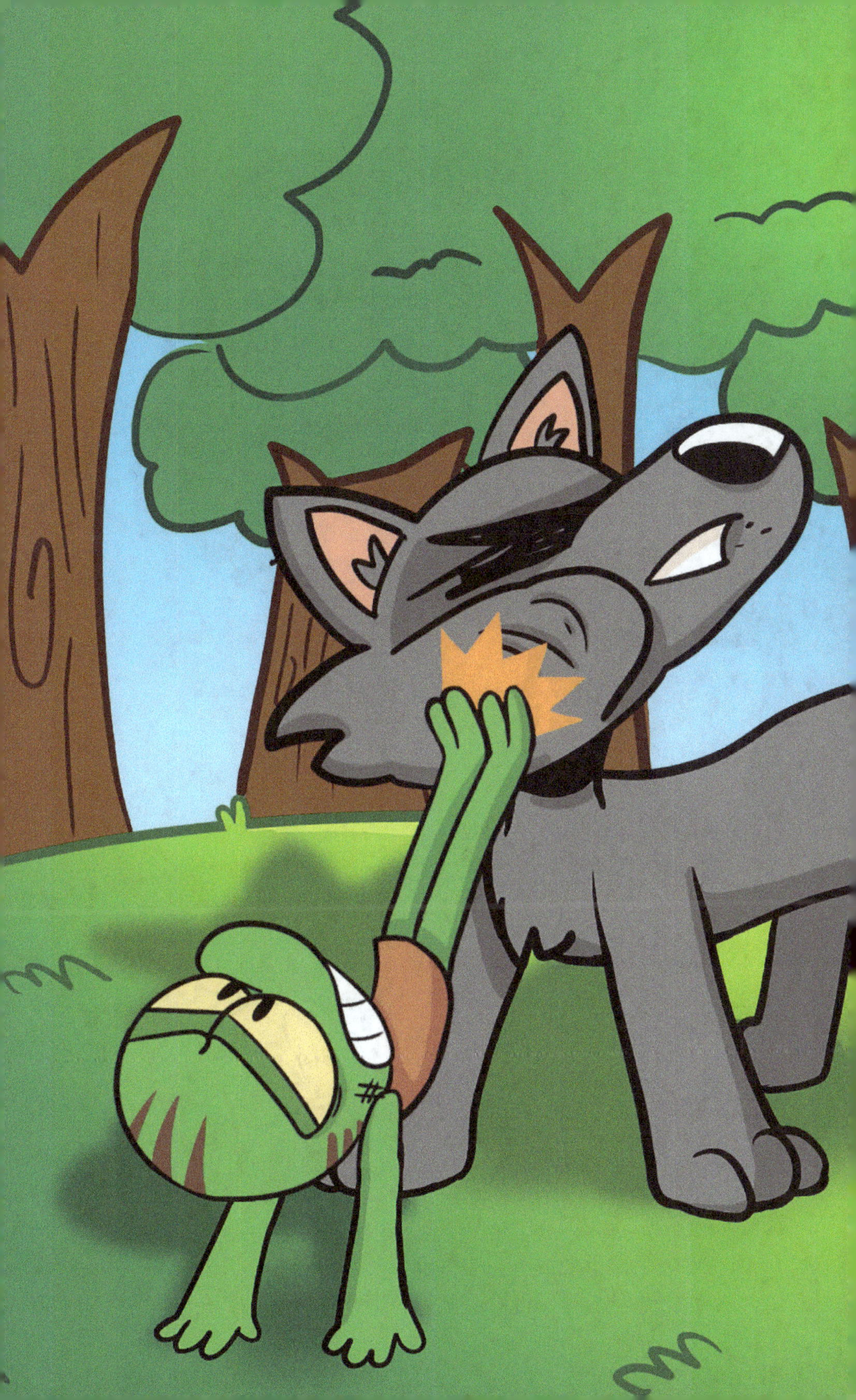

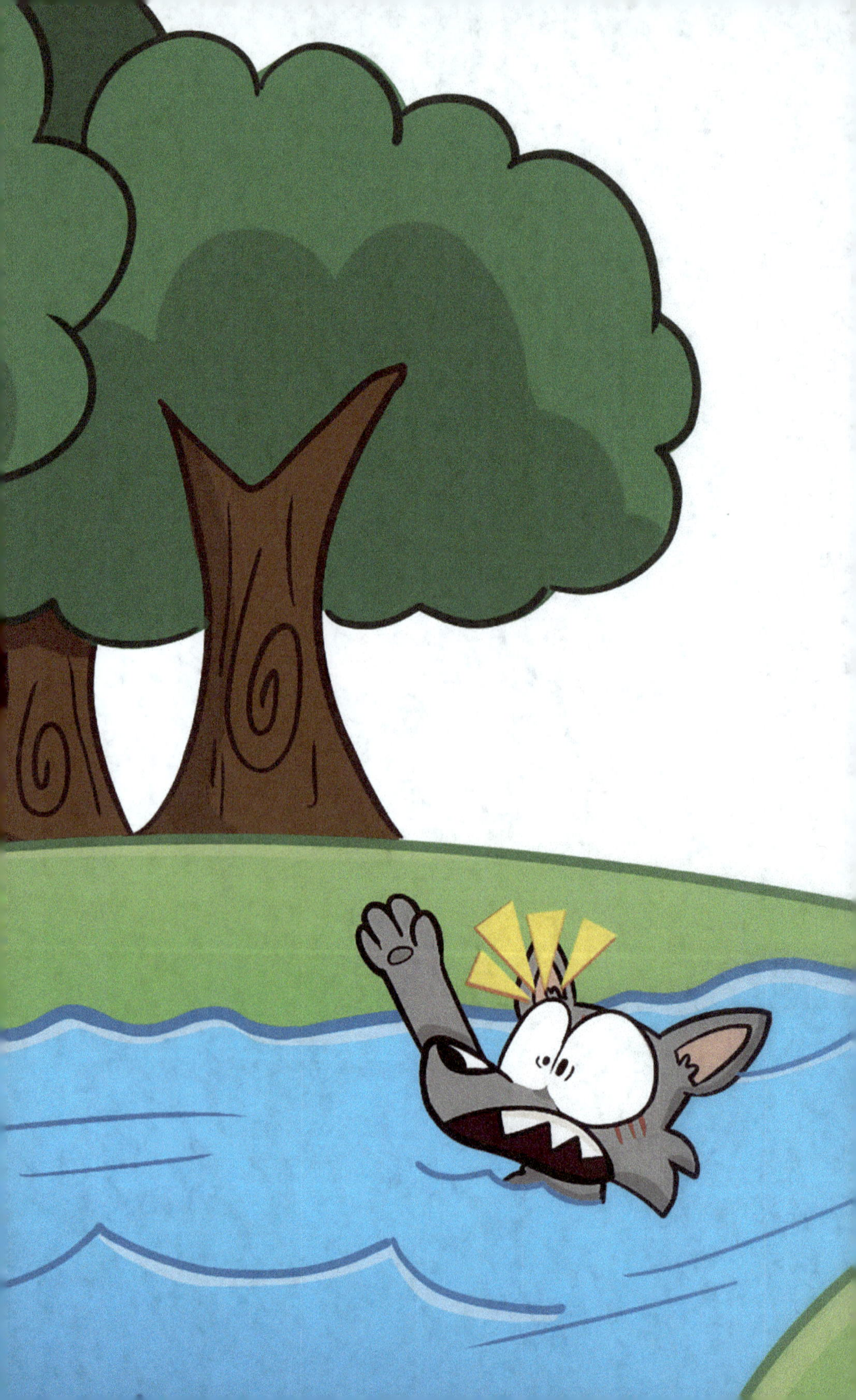

Scar was furious and attacked with force, but Frogie was able to jump and make him fall into the river, watching how the current carried him away.

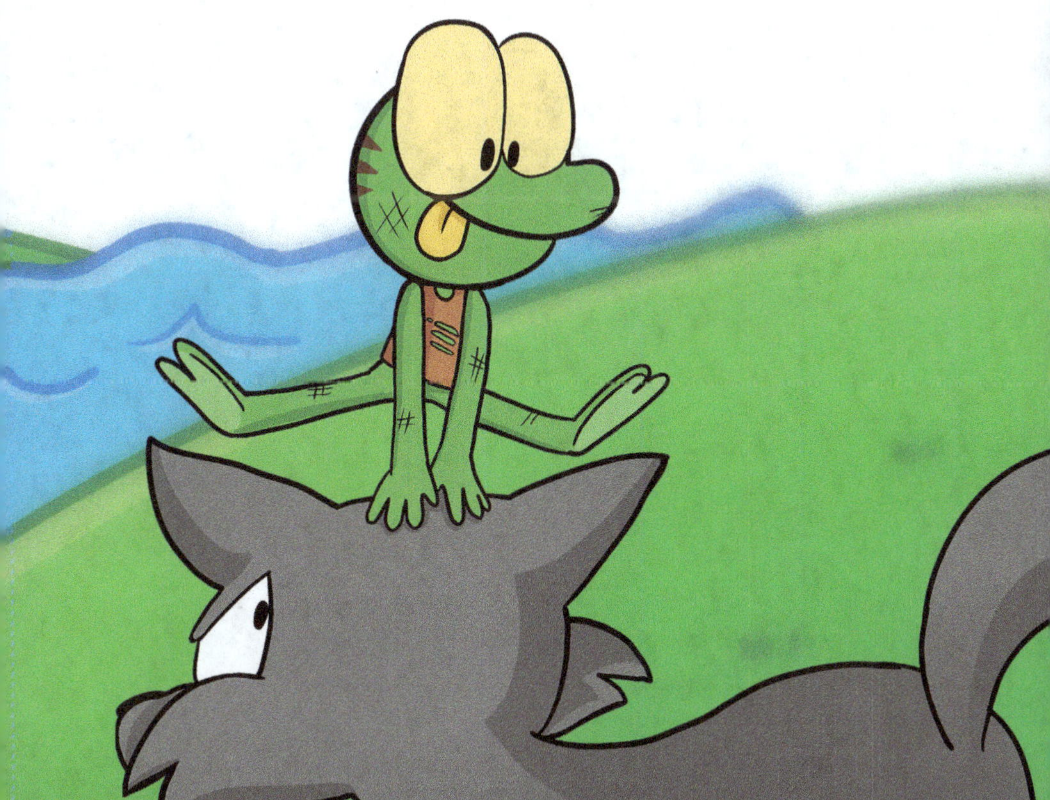

Frogie immediately went to check on his friend Laly, who had been found and cared for by her family. She woke up and asked him:

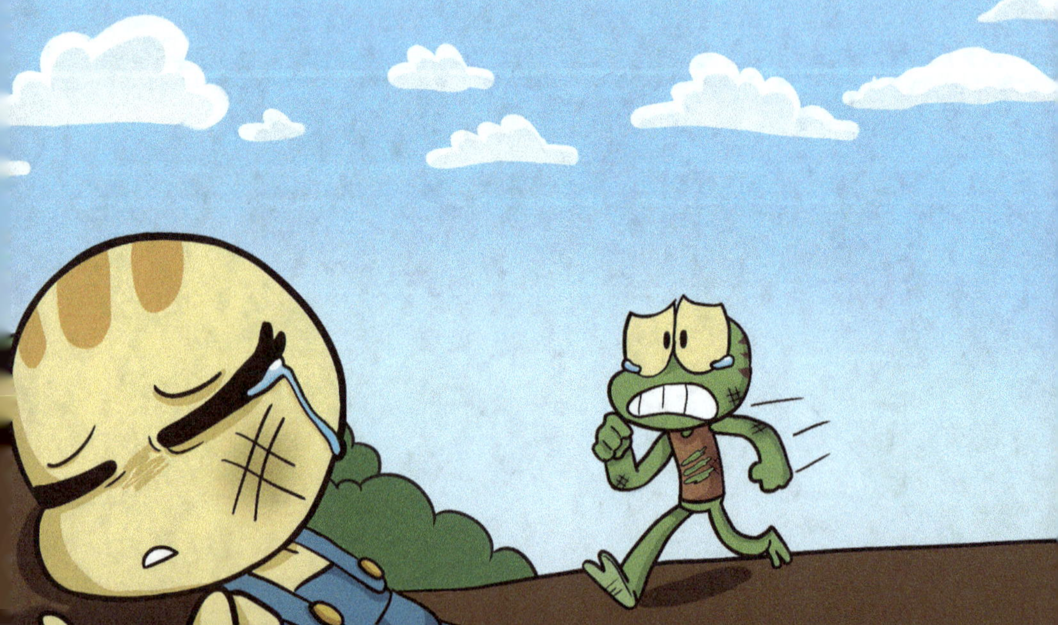

- Where is the coyote? Frogie replied:
-"I finally managed to win, dear friend, but this time in the presence of the whole kingdom".

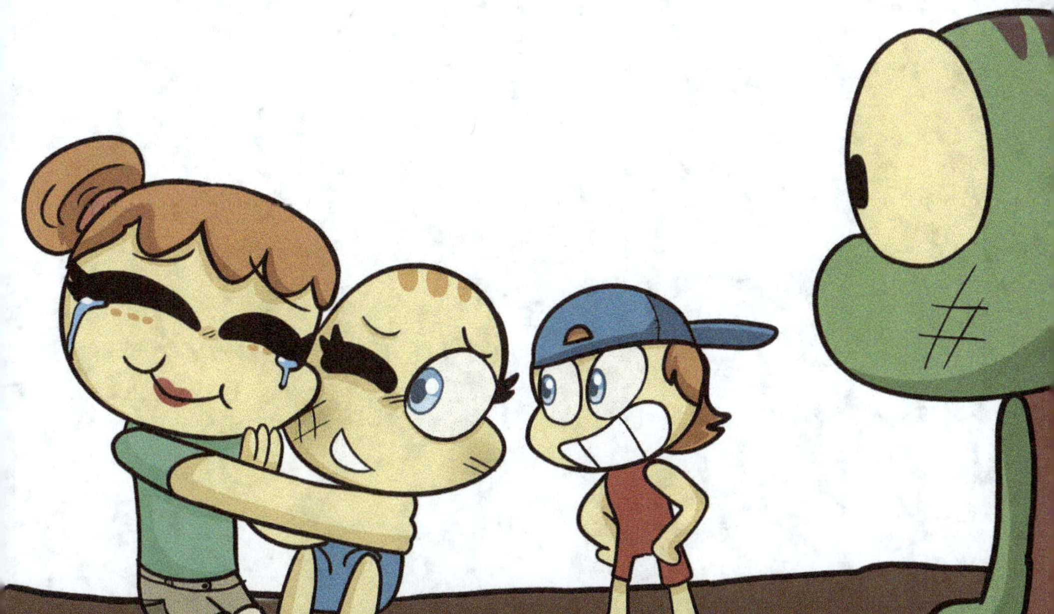

Everyone praised him and expressed their gratitude for his bravery and love. Frogie became the guardian and hero of the kingdom of Ranicor, and everyone respected and admired him for his noble character

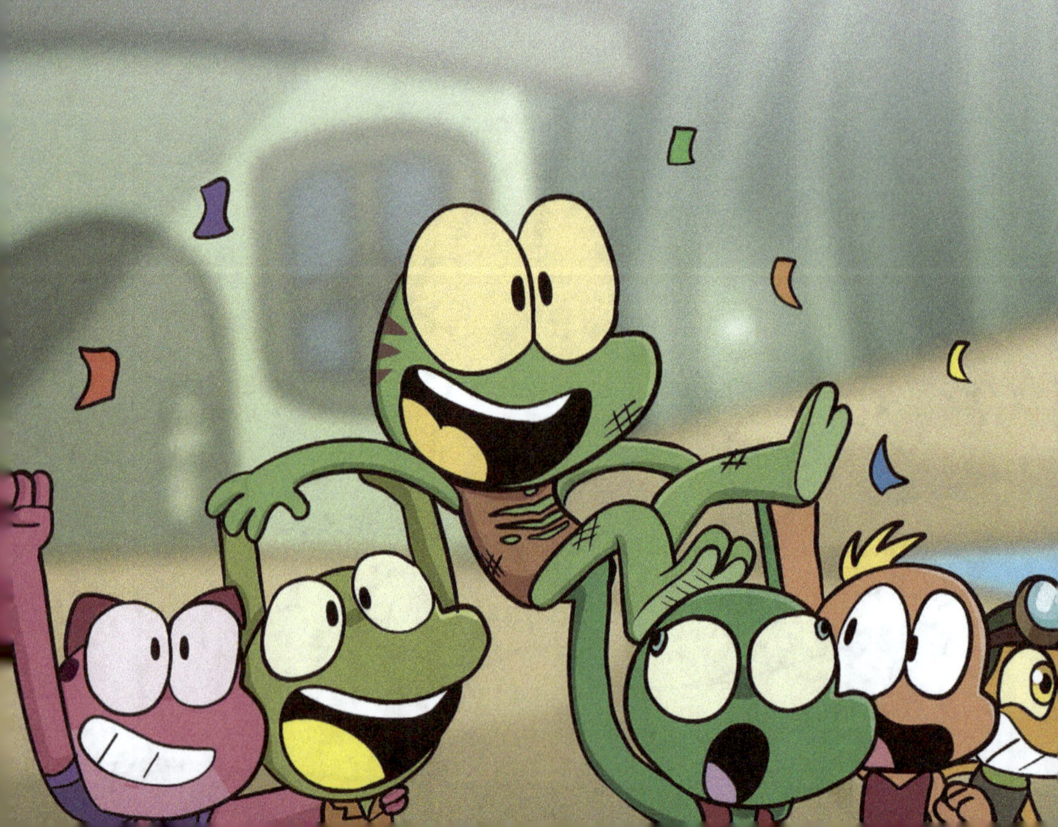

and love for the kingdom. After the
king fulfilled his promise and named
him a hero of Ranicor, he gave him
a beautiful palace.

It was celebrated with a big party
and he received the recognition he
had wanted so much.

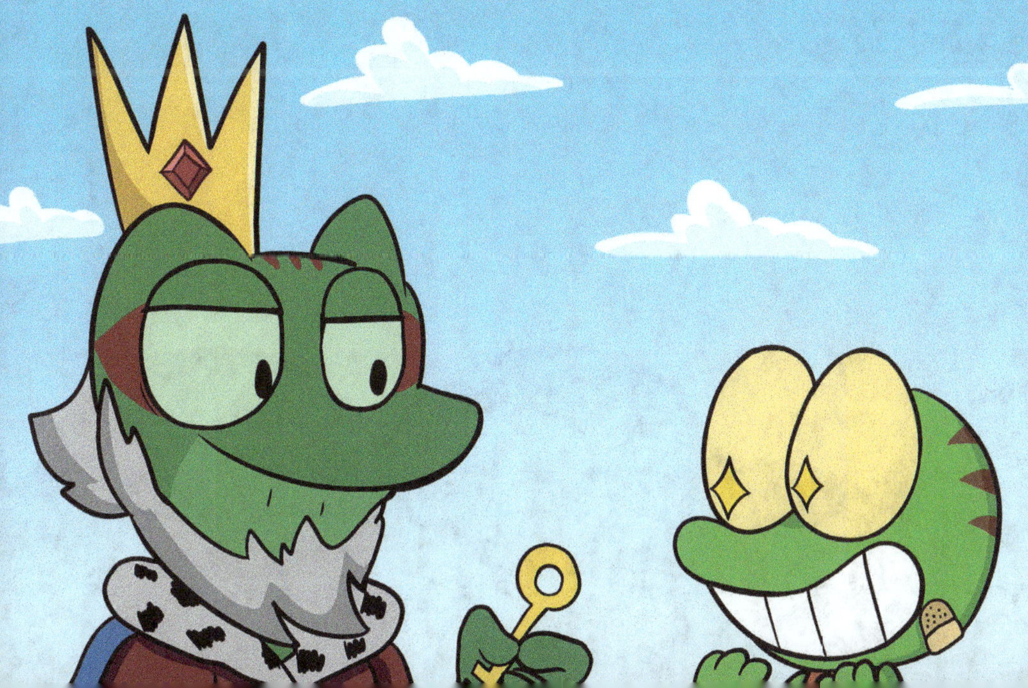

He became a symbol of inspiration to all the people of Ranicor and continued to protect those beautiful valleys with courage and dedication.

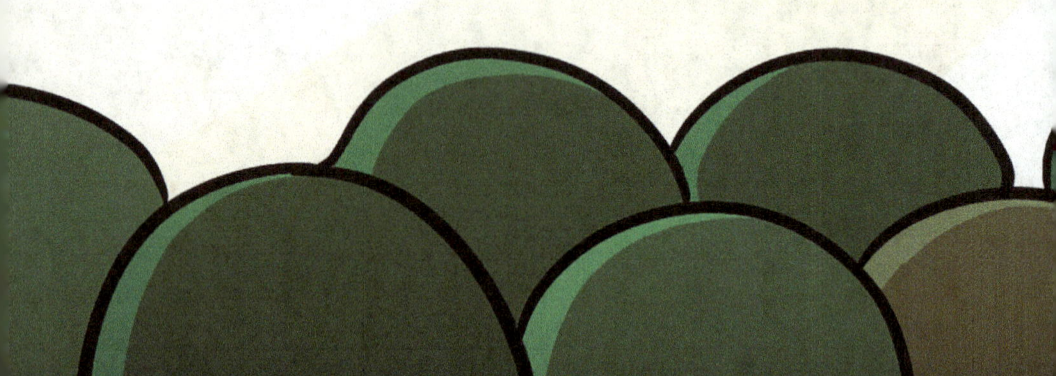

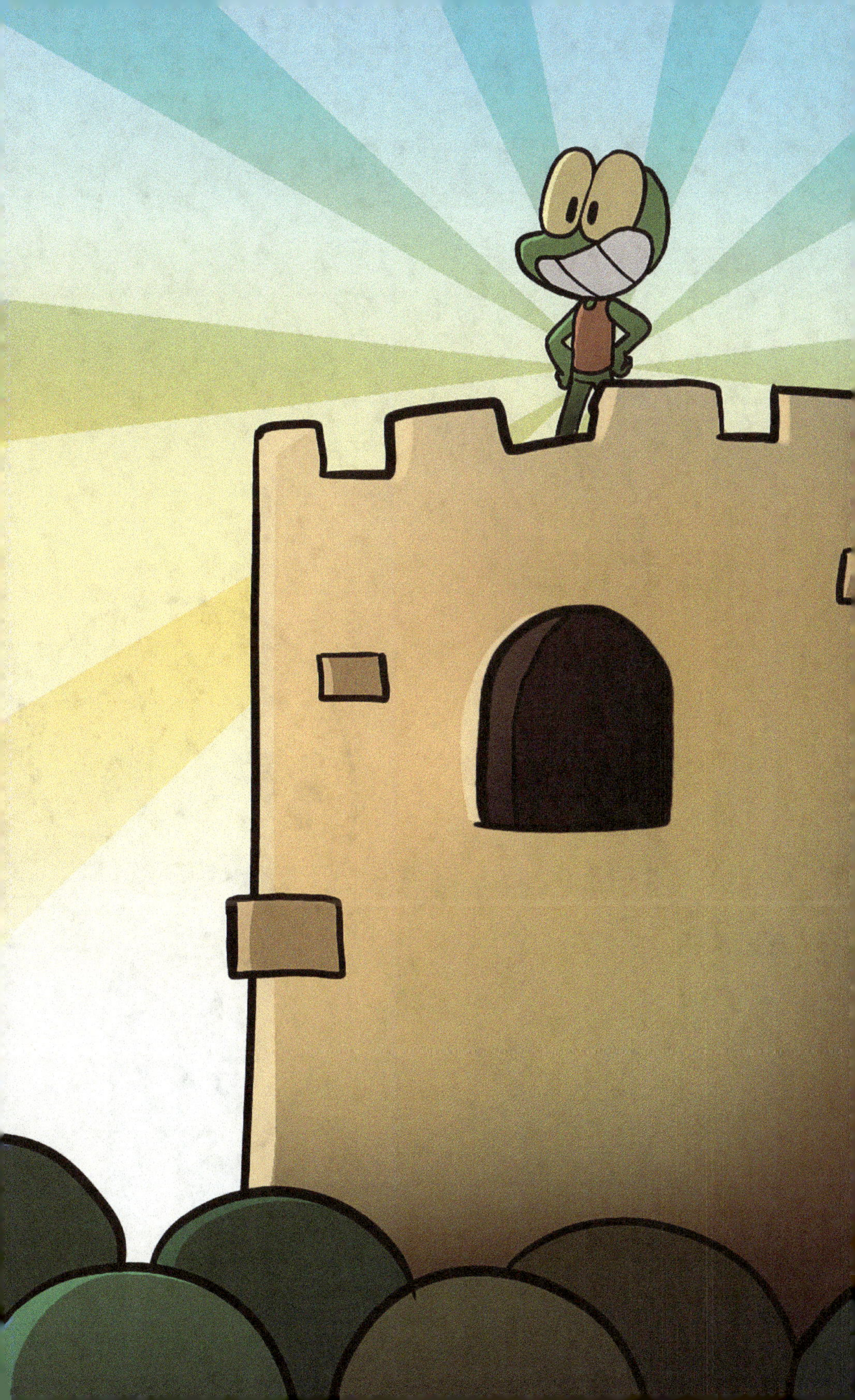

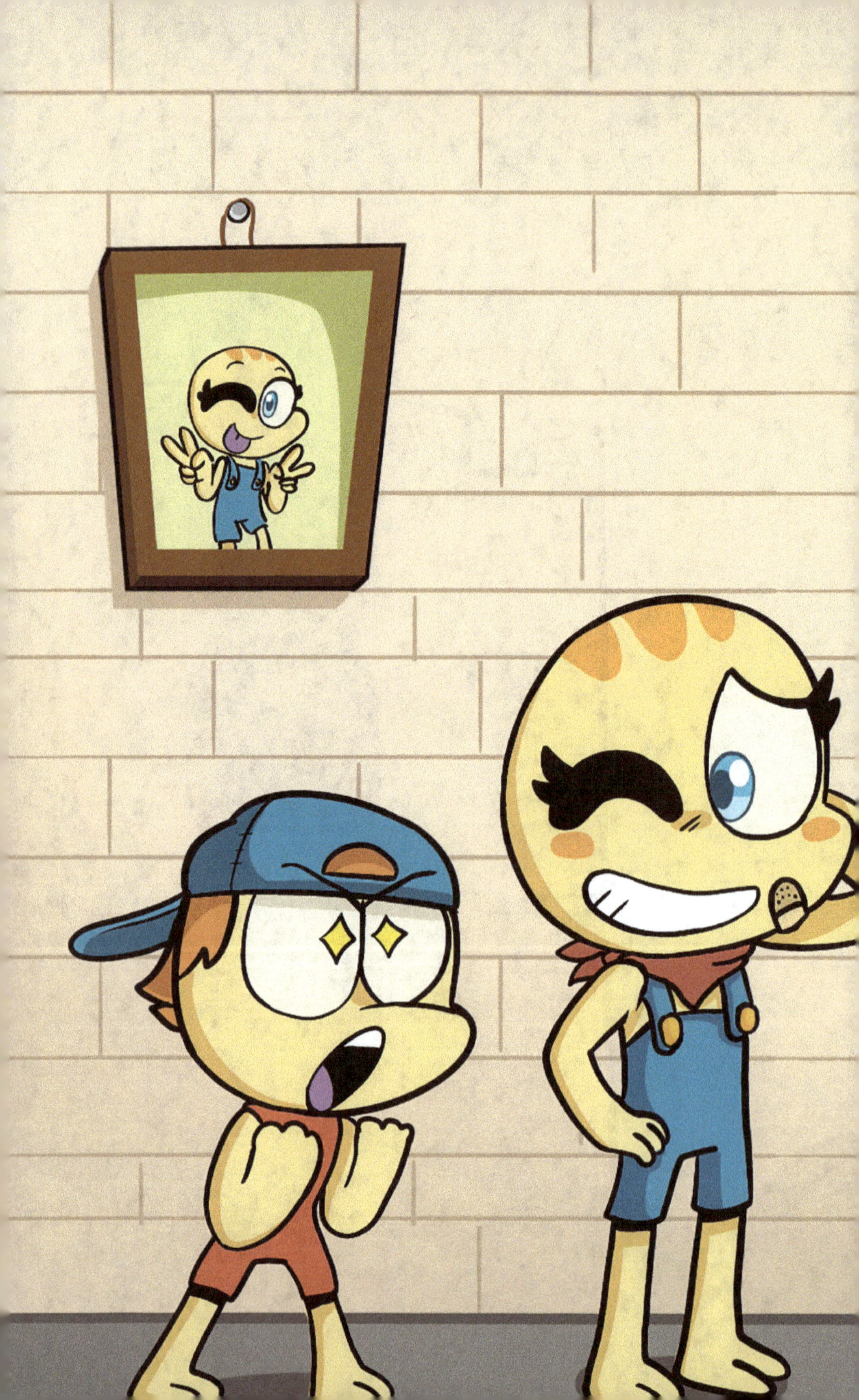

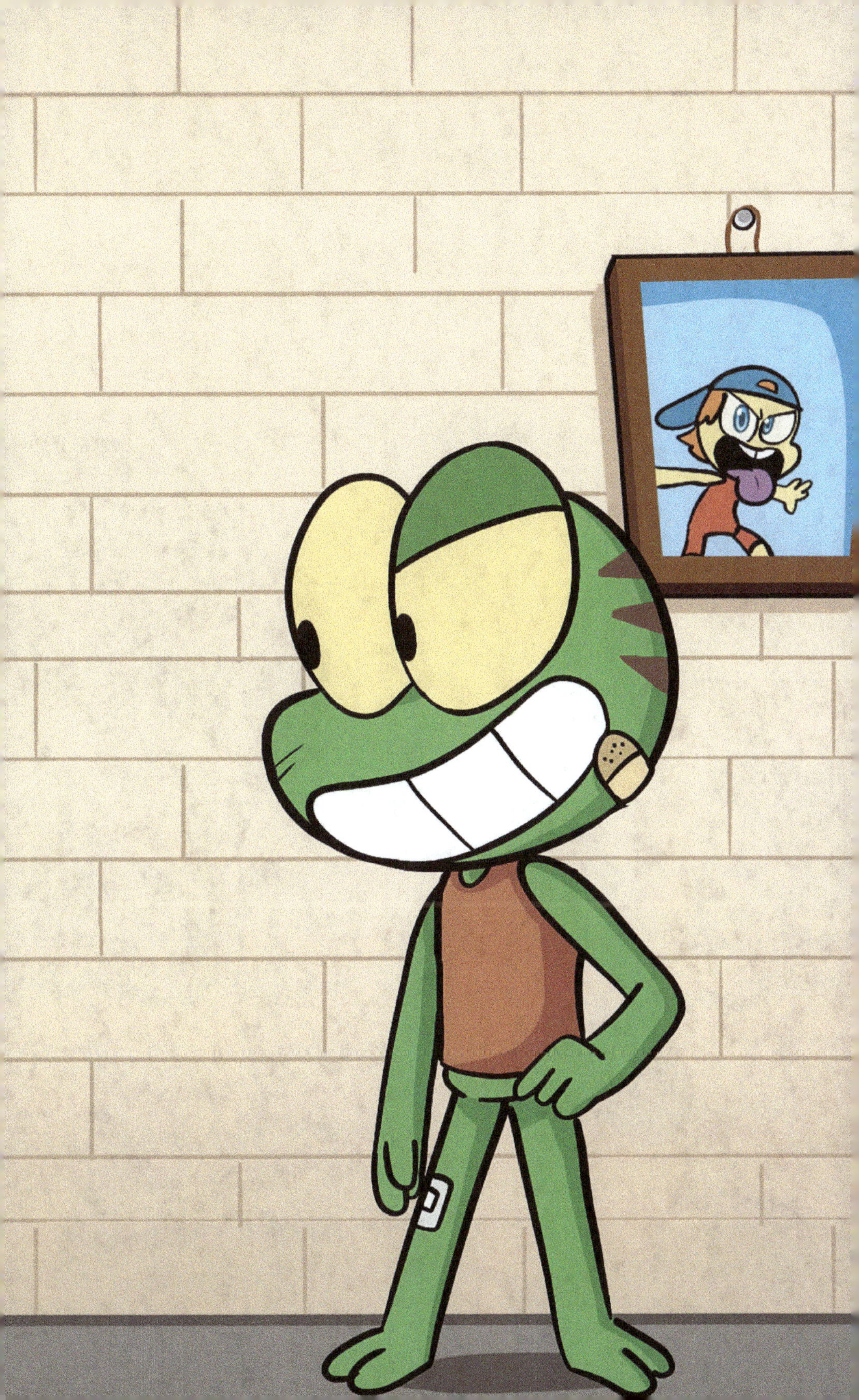

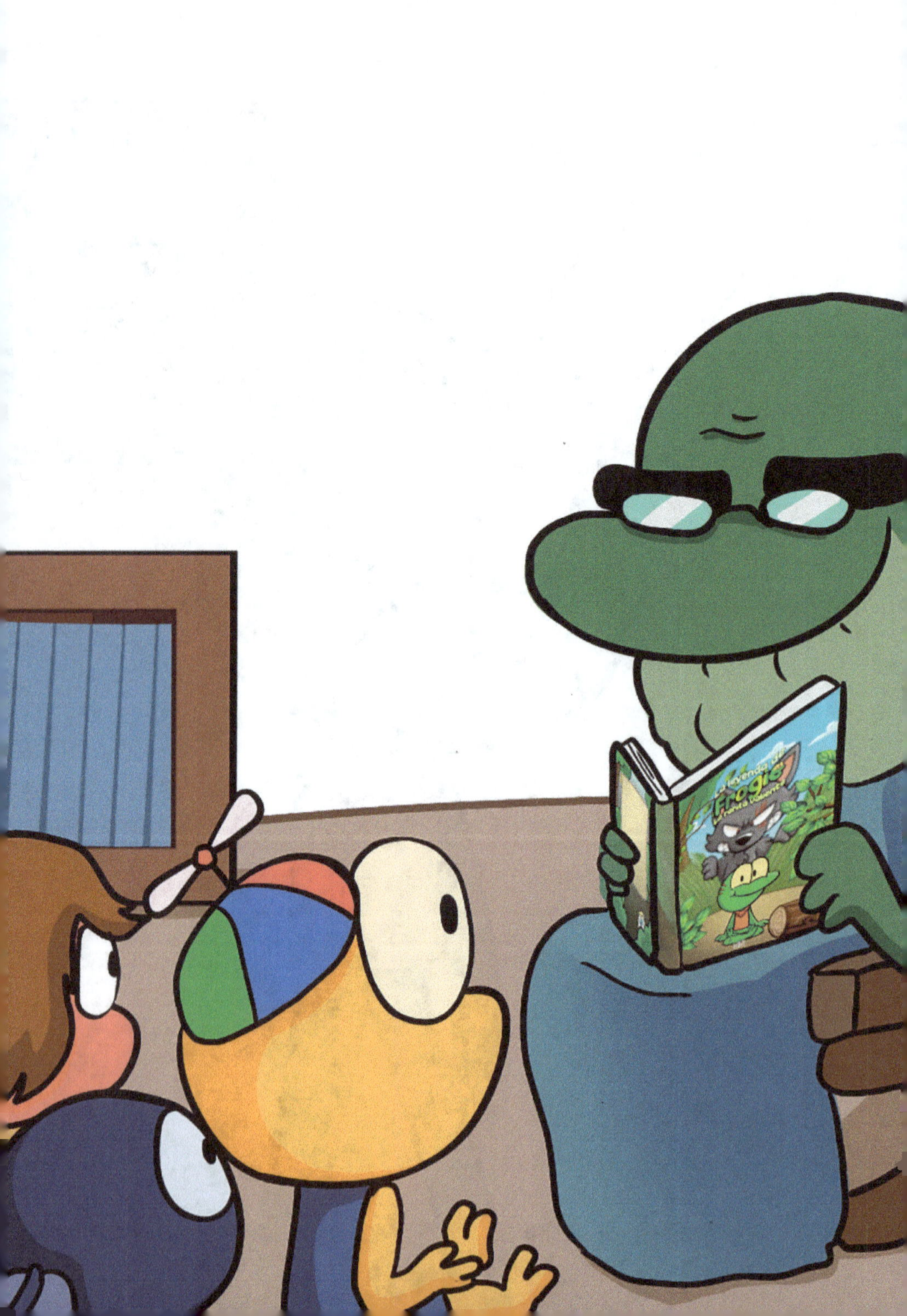
La leyenda de
Frogis

And so, his story became the legend of the brave little frog that will always be remembered in the kingdom of frogs. A legend that was passed down from generation to generation.

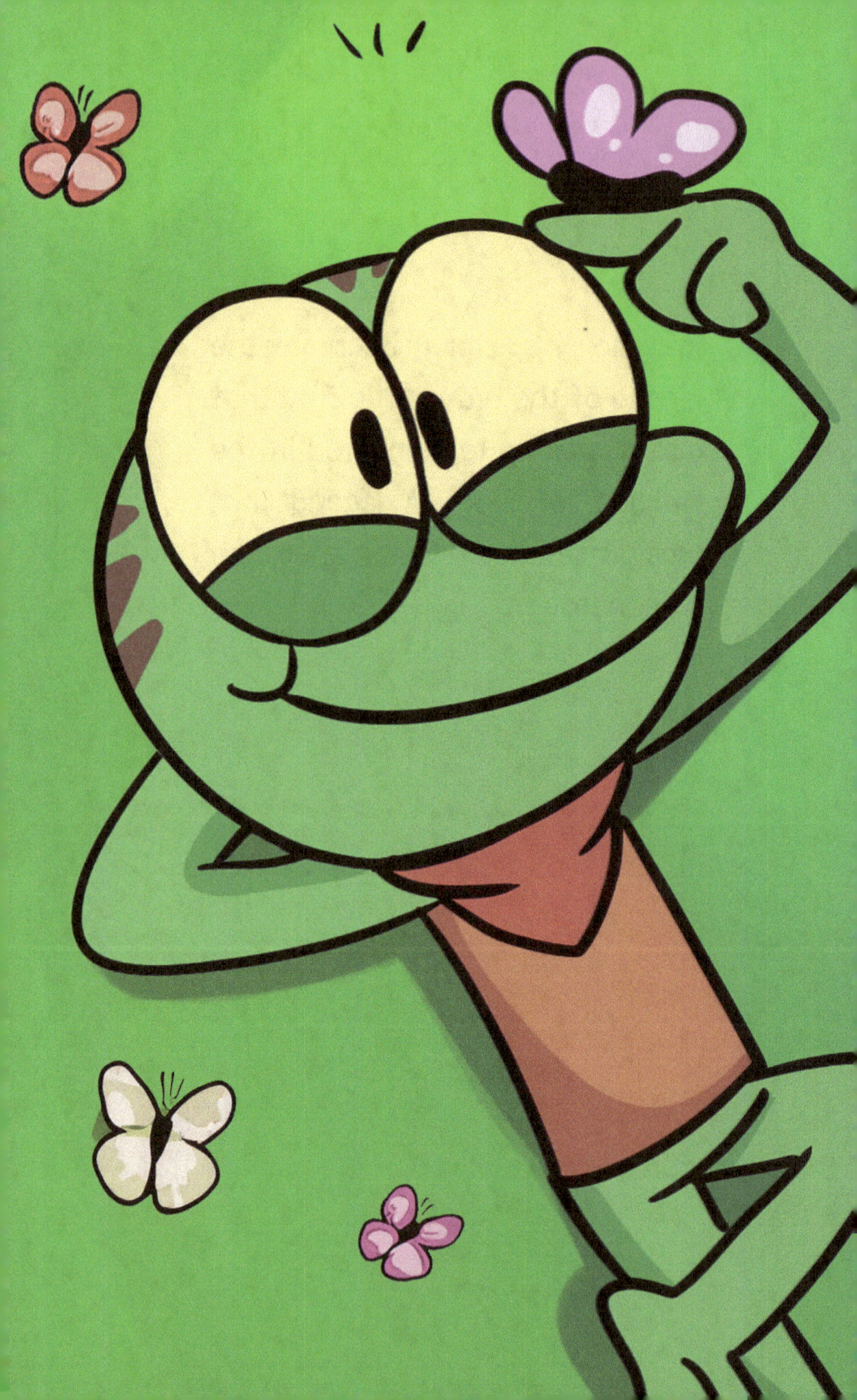

And so, knowing that his dream of becoming the hero of the frog kingdom had come true, he lived a happy life for the rest of his days. Frogie discovered that no matter how small or weak you are, you can always do great things if you have courage and tenacity.

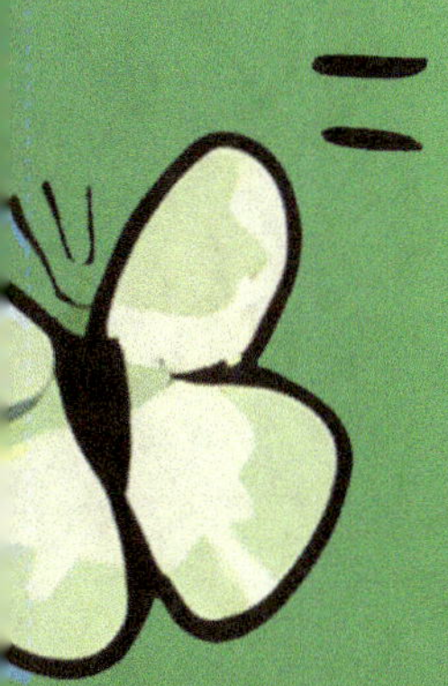

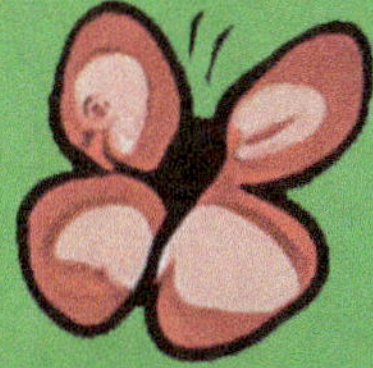

All Ranicor residents find inspiration
in him and he continued to protect
that beautiful valley with love and
dedication.

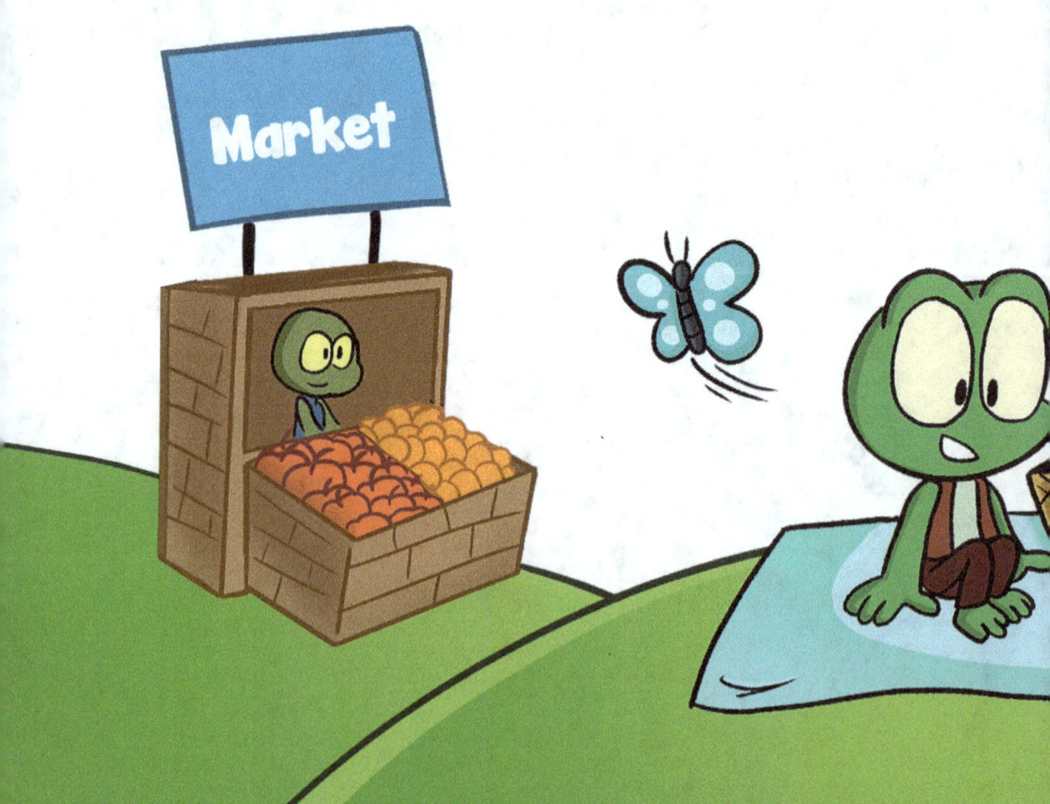

And so, his story became the brave little frog that will always be remembered in the kingdom of frogs, a story that was passed from generation to generation.

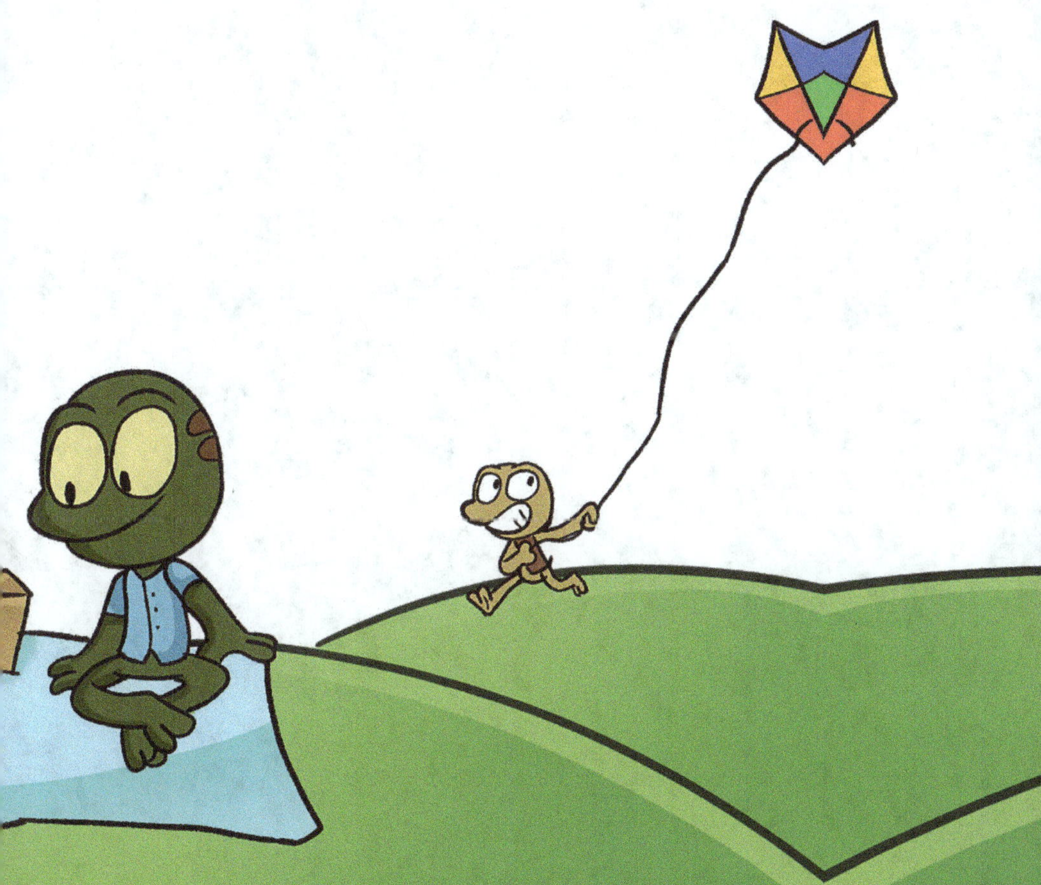

DIEGO
CARTOON

luisleo

www.soyfrogie.com

@soyfrogie

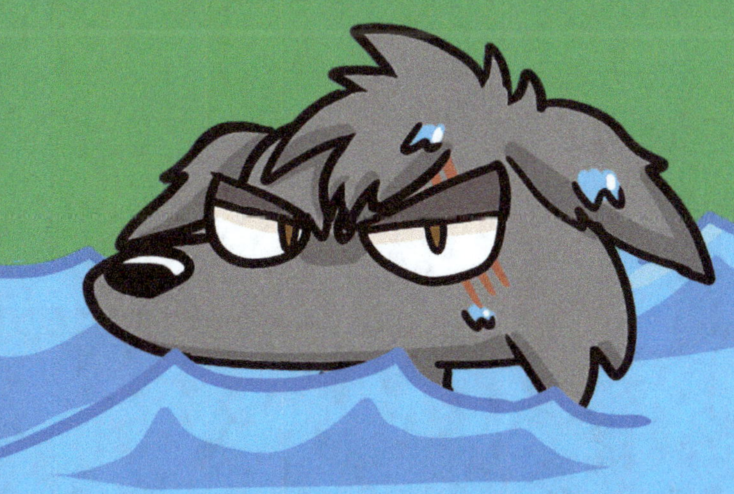

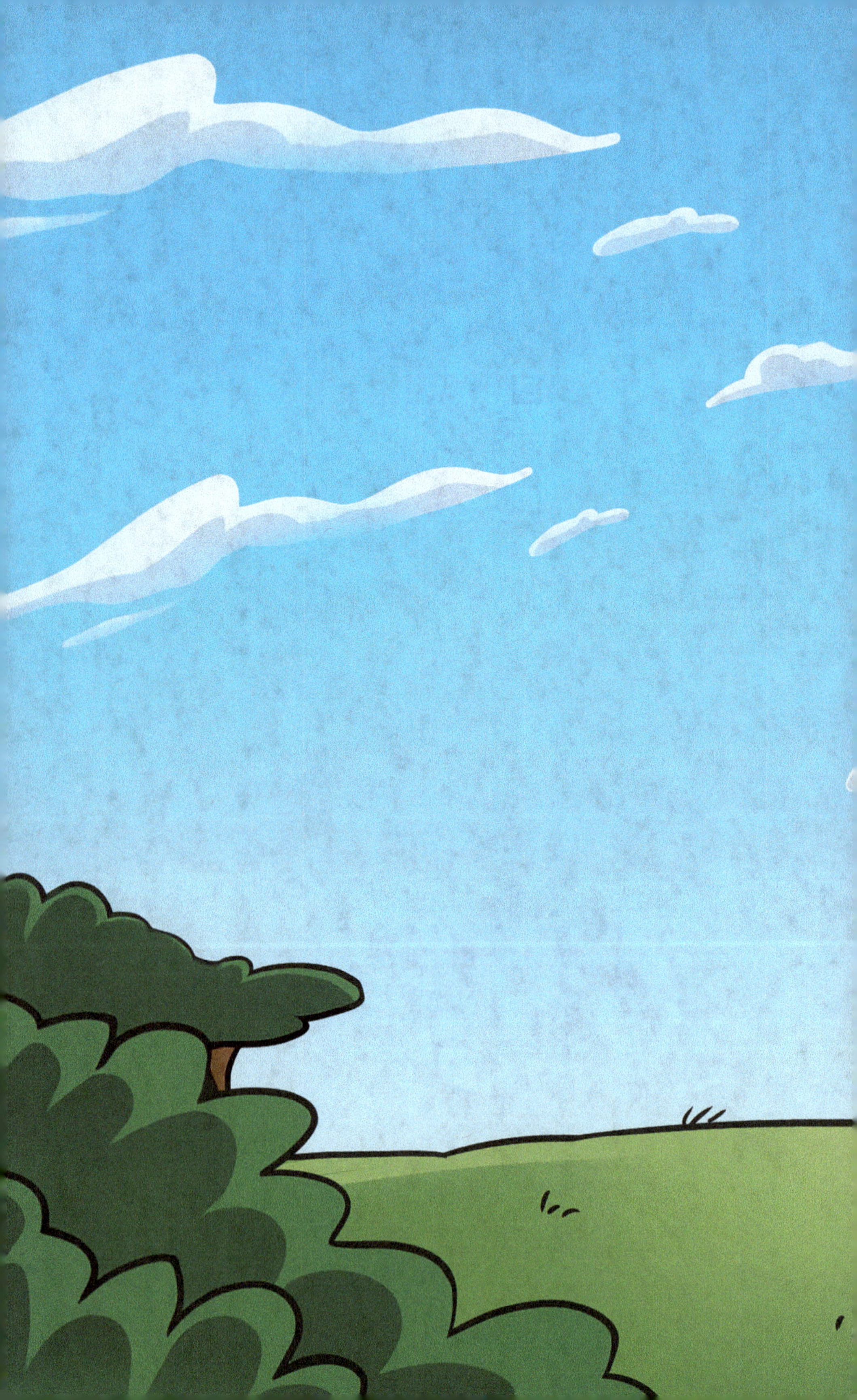

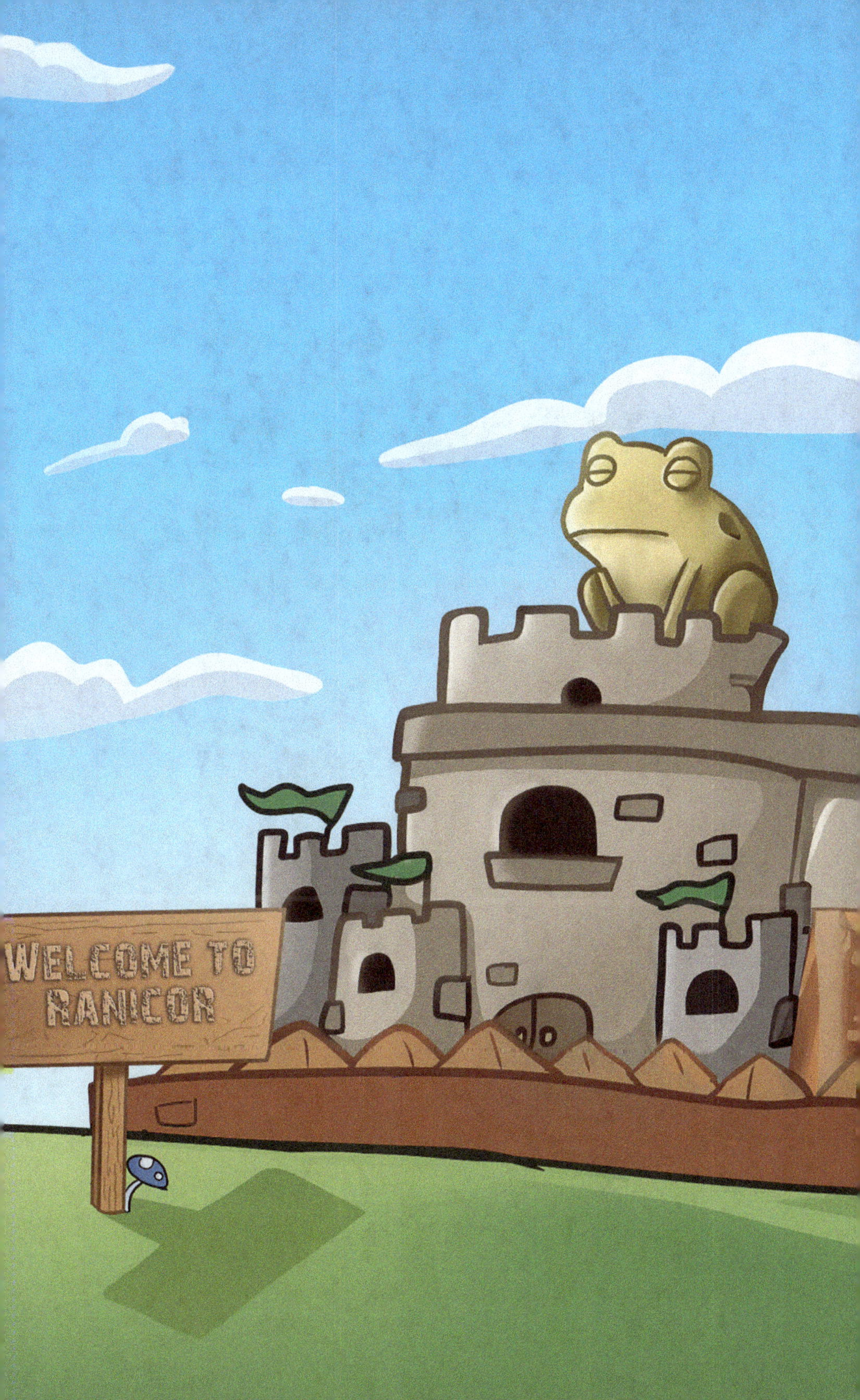

WELCOME TO
RANICOR

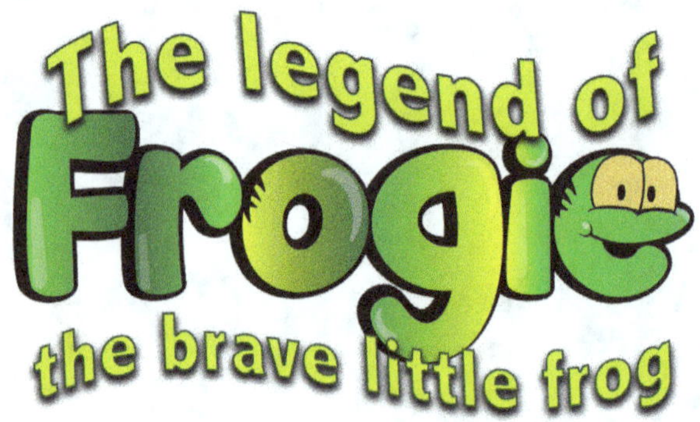

The legend of
Frogie
the brave little frog

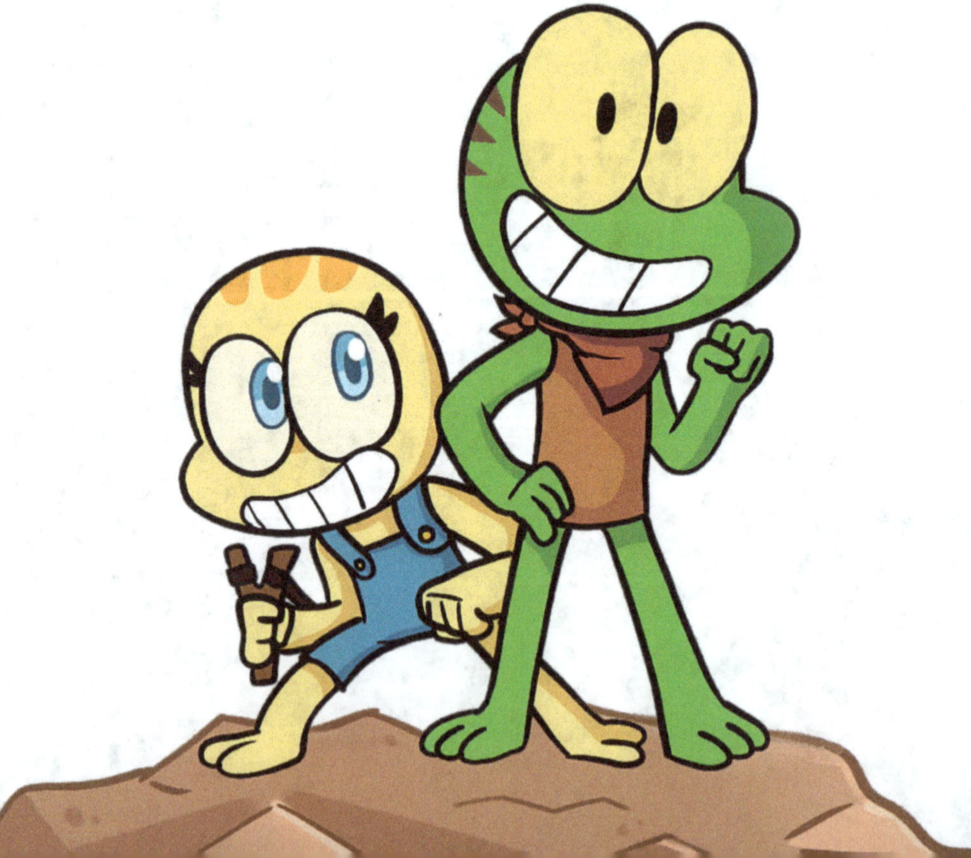